Modern Day Slavery

Nour E. Benakezouh

Copyright © 2024 Nour E. Benakezouh

All Rights Reserved

ISBN:

Acknowledgment

To my late parents, Messaoud & Fatima, who taught me to never give up fighting slavery, racism & injustice.

To my sons Tarik and Assirem, to whom I apologize, once again, for making them pay for my convictions.
I hope that they will be able to understand one day why I have done what and that they will never have to live what I survived.

To the Angolan young girl, whatever her name is and wherever she is today, whose father had thought that he had done the best thing for her by letting go with Dr Diallo to Bamako hoping that she would have the chance to go to school and build a bright future.

To Djamel Kaci, a true friend, without whom this book would never have seen the light of day. I hope this doesn't go to his head.

Modern Day Slavery

> *Despite the good we have done, the image of what we have not been able to do comes to disturb our satisfaction*
>
> - Sophie Cottin

On February 25, 2021 I had to undergo a delicate surgical procedure. At 7:23 a.m., as I was waiting to be taken to the operating room of the Montreal General Hospital, an image that I wasn't expecting came to haunt me.

I spent the night preceding the day of my surgery thinking of all the people I would have liked to have by my side before I walked through the doors of the operating room. My two children, Tarik & Assirem, were part of every scenario.

At no time during that night could I have guessed what would happen to me the following day. A day that became, by force of circumstances, one of the most memorable days of my life. Indeed, to my great surprise, it was a little Angolan girl whom I had the misfortune to know in Mali in 2008, during a one-year stint as an administration officer at the World Health Organization representation in Bamako, who stole the show from my two children.

I said that I had the misfortune to know her not because of what she had done to me but for the aftereffect that our meeting had on the rest of my life. I would have given everything that is dear to me not to live that episode of my life or, rather, for this episode to never have seen the day.

I am convinced that the little Angolan girl didn't intend to steal the spotlight from my children out of malice but much more because she wanted me to finish a job that I had started 13 years earlier. A job that I had not finished because of the vagaries of modern life. I do not say this to absolve myself but to reflect the sad reality that I leave you to appreciate throughout the reading of this book.

I really didn't know why she was there and what she was doing since she didn't, at any time, address a single word to me, but I knew one thing very well: I knew that I owed her, at the very least, an apology. An apology for not having been able to free her from the modern-day slavery in which she had found herself, not in the hands of a colonist but in the hands of a native like her.

In addition to whispering sorry to her, once again that day, I made her a promise that I will do everything in my power to expose the person who had treated her like a modern-day slave and all the people who, for one reason or another, chose to turn a blind eye to the way she was treated.

After asking her for forgiveness, I asked her to pray for me so that I would return safe and sound from this surgery. In return, I committed to her to finish my work.

During that time period that seemed like an eternity, I had forgotten everything, even the danger of the surgical intervention that awaited me. I hoped for only one thing: that the little Angolan girl would find it in her heart to forgive me because I didn't succeed in my attempt to free her. Only God knows that I had done everything I could and knew how to do to give her hope and make her believe in humanity.

The writing of this book, after having used all the means available to me, is part of the promise I made to the little girl, whose name I never knew and whose destiny I am unaware of to this day.

I will soon undergo another surgical procedure in the same operating room of the same hospital, and at the hands of the same surgeon, Dr Ahmed Aoude. I don't know if the little Angolan girl will decide to accompany me to the operating room as she did in 2021. If so, I will be able to look her in the eye and say: *"I kept my promise"*.

If it is not the case, I do not lose hope of seeing her again one day. I will ask her for her name and tell her in person: I have kept my promise, although I took my time to do so. Better late than never.

Nour E. Benakezouh

*I have a dream, a song to sing
To help me cope with anything*

- The ABBA

In a press release dated June 18th, 2020 and signed by the World Health Organization (WHO), UNICEF, UNESCO, the Special Representative of the Secretary-General of the United Nations on Violence against Children and the Partnership for the Elimination of Violence, considered it useful and necessary to bring to the attention of the whole world the conclusions of the **"Status report on the prevention of violence against children worldwide."**

In their press release, these organizations did not just talk about the report in question; they went further by calling on the public authorities to take further action.

Indeed, after having brought to our attention that *"every year, one child in two in the world - or around a billion children - is a victim of acts of physical, sexual or psychological violence that led to trauma, disabilities or even death,"* these organizations have even pointed out the source of the problem, namely the lack of will of countries that fail to implement the strategies established to protect children.

Dr Tedros Adhanom Ghebreyesus, WHO Director-General, was very categorical on the issue of violence against children. He stated unequivocally that, *"Children must not be victims of violence under any circumstances. We have evidence-based tools to prevent this violence, and we call on all countries to use them. Safeguarding the health and well-being of children is essential to safeguarding the health and well-being of all, now and in the future."*

Dr. Tedros Adhanom Ghebreyesus, however, forgot one crucial thing in his speech to convince countries to use the tools at their disposal. He forgot to say to the whole world whether the WHO had used these tools. This omission was deliberate on his part because he did not have the courage to tell the truth. This bitter truth is he forgot to use these tools, or rather didn't care enough to use these tools to prevent, first, and then fight against violence against children by senior WHO officials within his own organization. It would have been much easier for him to convince countries to use his tools if he had taken the care to use them himself in his organization: the World Health Organization.

Indeed, fifteen months later, more precisely on Tuesday, September 28, 2021, the Director General of the WHO returned to the world press to speak, this time, about what happened within his organization in terms of sexual exploitation.

Instead of spending fortunes to collaborate with countries to fully implement INSPIRE strategies, these organizations, led by WHO, should have tried to convince by example and not by words. As they say, **"True charity begins at home."**

If the World Health Organization had used its own tools, its representative in the Bamako office would never have dared to bring back from Luanda a thirteen-year-old girl whom she had deprived of schooling and whom she had used like a modern-day slave.

If the World Health Organization had used its own tools, WHO Director-General Dr. Tedros Adhanom Ghebreyesus would never have to hold a press conference on September 28, 2021, to address victims and survivors who had suffered the sexual exploitation and abuse described in the report of the Commission of Inquiry into Allegations of Sexual Exploitation and Abuse during the response to the Tenth Ebola Virus Disease Outbreak in North Kivu and Ituri Provinces, Democratic Republic of the Congo.

If the World Health Organization had used its own tools, WHO Director-General Dr. Tedros Adhanom Ghebreyesus would not have to feel sorry for what the victims and the survivors of sexual exploitation and abuse suffered at the hands of people who were employed by WHO and for the lasting suffering these events caused.

During this same conference, Dr. Tedros Adhanom Ghebreyesus did something that impressed me the first time I read his statement in the French daily newspaper "Le Monde" on September 28th, 2021.

He declared: *"My top priority is to ensure that the perpetrators of these acts do not go unpunished and that they are held accountable."*

As I am no longer naive and cannot afford to be it at my age, I went, just after reading the article in Le Monde, to the WHO website to read the speech of the WHO Director-General and the final report of the independent commission to review allegations of sexual exploitation and abuse committed during the response to the tenth outbreak of the Ebola virus disease, DRC.

I was delighted to read Dr. Tedros Adhanom Ghebreyesus upholding that: *"As Director-General, I ultimately bear responsibility for the behavior of the people we employ and for any failures in the system that allowed that behavior to happen."*

As soon as I finished reading the speech of the WHO DG and the final report of the independent commission, I tried to find out if Dr. Diallo was still working for the WHO.

Modern Day Slavery

To my great surprise, I learned that Dr. Diallo was the WHO representative in Lomé, Togo. I immediately realized the mistake I had made in trying to find out certain things on my 62nd birthday. I should have waited a day or two and not taken the risk of ruining my birthday.

Torn between the WHO Director-General's statement that: *"As Director-General, I ultimately bear responsibility for the behavior of the people we employ and for any system failures that allowed that behavior,"* and the reality of learning that Dr. Diallo was still working at WHO, I willingly let my eternal optimism have the last word.

Indeed, the experience of learning that Dr. Diallo was still employed by the WHO was very painful since it made me relive all the nightmares that I had experienced in 2008 and which I still could not get over because I failed in my mission to put an end to the exploitation of a little Angolan girl, the daughter of a driver at the WHO representation in Luanda, an orphan of her mother, whom Dr. Diallo had brought back with her from Angola, following her assignment in Bamako in January 2008.

Completely devastated by this latest information, I called, once again and not for the last time, upon my optimism to find the last joules of energy I needed to write a letter that same day to the WHO DG in which I told him the story of the little Angolan girl.

Although my friends were pessimistic when I told them about my decision to refer the matter to the WHO DG, once again, my desire to give the runner a second chance to prove to us what he was capable of and what he was made of, he who had ended his speech on September 28, 2021, by stating: *"As Director-General, I ultimately take responsibility for the behavior of the people we employ and for any failures in the system that allowed this behavior.*

And I will take personal responsibility for doing what is necessary to prevent this from happening again," got the better of me.

I must admit that my optimism in this matter has always been supported by the fact that I was tired of having to continually account for myself to my conscience, which has never stopped questioning me. I therefore preferred to act in this matter rather than having to regularly account for myself to my conscience.

In addition to wanting to do justice to the little Angolan girl and to avoid having to answer to my conscience, I also wanted to indirectly help the WHO DG in his effort to remove this black stain that was now on the name of his organization. Having worked for the WHO, I considered that this stain was also on my personal name. Indeed, when people talked about sexual exploitation within the WHO, I always felt concerned even though I had only worked for the WHO for one year, and that was 16 years ago. How time flies.

Having seen nothing coming, despite the promises made to me on October 7th, 2021, by Ms. Cristiana Fascetto, an investigator in the WHO Office of Internal Oversight Services (IOS), in an email in which she informed me that she was the person responsible for investigating any allegations concerning WHO staff. She wanted me to know that since my allegations were very serious, her office proceeded to immediately open an investigation.

I sent a second letter to the WHO DG on December 18, 2022, when I discovered by pure chance that Ms. Fascetto didn't work for the WHO since May 2022.

The person who replaced her, Mr. Tarik Ottmani, never felt the need to bring this fact to my attention. He, who dared to talk about transparency the first time I had to speak to him as part of the investigation, kept his lips sealed when transparency did not suit him. For Mr. Ottmani, transparency is a one-way mirror; it applied to me but not to him.

On May 12, 2023, I sent a third letter to the WHO DG to express my disappointment in light of what has happened since October 1, 2021, the date of my first letter. I brought to his attention facts that I cannot disclose because of the non-disclosure agreement I had signed with WHO before the investigation began.

Almost three years later, I realized that the promise of the WHO DG was not worth $250, the amount that WHO had awarded to each survivor of sexual exploitation and abuse committed by WHO employees in the DRC.

I also noted that the Director-General of the World Health Organization made his promise of 28 September 2021 as part of his election campaign for a second term at the head of WHO. Dr Tedros Adhanom Ghebreyesus was appointed at the Seventy-fifth World Health Assembly in May 2022, on the proposal of the Executive Board. May 2022 is also, by coincidence, the month Ms. Cristiana Fascetto was let go by WHO. Which goes to show that it is not safe to know more than you need to when you work at the WHO.

At this stage of the WHO game, I lost all confidence in the WHO "investigation." Doubts as to the seriousness of the latter finally took hold of me.

I would even say more; I was convinced that WHO, contrary to what I was led to believe, had no intention of conducting an investigation. The WHO's higher authorities knew exactly what had happened in Bamako in 2008 since I had brought to the attention of the former Director-General Dr. Margaret Chan all the facts, with supporting evidence and documents. They, therefore, did not need an investigation that would lead them to where they already were.

I had and have no reason to believe that Ms. Fascetto lied to me on October 7, 2021, when she literally told me:

"Your letter of October 1st to the Director-General has been forwarded to our office. As the allegations you reported are very serious, we proceeded to immediately open an investigation."

To this day I have no reason to doubt her honesty or question her good faith when she wrote what she wrote to me. I even think that her honesty is probably behind the fact that she is no longer with the WHO since May 2022.

My loss of confidence was due to the lack of transparency since the WHO had hidden from me the exclusion of Ms. Cristiana Fascetto from this investigation and the type of questions that were asked of me by the person who had replaced her.

I discovered Ms. Cristiana Falsettos' departure from the WHO by pure chance. Seeing nothing moving more than a year after the investigation was opened, I sent her an email to find out where things stood. To my great surprise, I received an email telling me that Ms. Fascetto was no longer with the WHO. In the email, I had been given the name of another person who did not want to tell me why Ms. Fascetto was no longer working at the WHO.

If the questions I was asked during the interview with the investigators are any indication, I was entitled to conclude that the investigators were in no way interested in understanding what happened in the WHO office in Bamako in 2008. If not, how can one explain the fact that no questions were asked of me concerning the reasons why Dr. Diallo was never questioned despite all her actions (exploitation, abuse of power, embezzlement, forgery, and use of forgery, defamation, etc.), that I had denounced and documented?

Modern Day Slavery

The only person who had inspired me with confidence in this "investigation" was Ms. Fascetto. Now that she is no longer part of the landscape and her sidelining had been hidden from me, I saw no reason to still pretend to believe. It turns out that she was removed from WHO in May 2022, just after the re-election of Dr. Tedros Adhanom Ghebreyesus. At no time did WHO consider it useful or necessary to communicate this information to me.

Once I had lost all faith in the WHO, I did something I do every time I hit a wall: listening to the song "I have a dream" by the Swedish group ABBA on repeat.

Luckily, I didn't have to pay royalties each time I listened to the song; I would be bankrupt by now if I did.

I knew there was only one cartridge left in my gun, but I didn't know what Tarik & Assirem would think now that they are adults.

In 2009, the same question arose for me: Should I publish a book so that everyone knows what is happening within the WHO? At the time, the answer was obvious: "No, it is out of the question."

I could not, for all the gold in the world, expose my children to any risk. I had just lost my job with the WHO because I could not condone the slavery of a 13-year-old girl. I couldn't sacrifice two other children, ages 9 and 11, my own, or make them pay the price for my beliefs. The fact that their father is unemployed is already too high a price to pay for them who would suffer the consequences of their father's job loss.

I was eager to hear my children's answers to the same question now that they are adults. Their answer did not surprise me at all. What did surprise me, however, was the speed with which they answered the question and the comment that followed their answer: "Dad, you waited too long."

Yes, I waited too long, but this wait was not by choice. I had no choice but to endure them. I hope that the little Angolan girl and my children will come to understand, one day, the position I found myself in.

Now that the decision to publish the book has been made, I took care to inform the Director-General of WHO by letter that I sent him on Friday, July 19, 2024. I did it out of politeness and to avoid any confusion. He was going to find out one day or another, and I preferred that he learn it from me.

Don't forget who will fill out your PMDS (Personnel Management and Development System)
- Dr. Fatoumata Binta Tidiane Diallo

On January 24, 2008, I met a person at the Modibo Keita International Airport in Bamako whose encounter changed the course of my life and my way of seeing and understanding the world.

As the Administration Officer of the WHO Representation in Bamako, I went to the airport to welcome the new WHO Representative in Bamako, Dre Fatoumata Binta Tidiane Diallo. She was arriving from Luanda, Angola, where she had been performing the same duties, to replace Dr. Lamine Cisse Saar, with whom I had spent two enjoyable months and who was assigned to fulfill the same duties at the WHO Representation in Nouakchott, Mauritania.

Upon disembarking from the plane, Dr. Diallo went to the VIP lounge, where a delegation from the WHO representation in Bamako was waiting to welcome her to Mali.

I didn't need more than two minutes with her to realize what kind of person I was going to watch over the interests of the WHO in Bamako. Indeed, after our introductions, Dr. Diallo wanted to know the score of the football game between her native country, Guinea Conakry, and Morocco, as part of the African Cup of Nations taking place in Ghana.

In order to break the ice, I told her that Guinea was leading but that it was going to lose given the way the match was going.

To my great surprise, she told me curtly: "*You should never forget who is going to prepare your PMDS (Personnel Management and Development System).*" This sentence remained engraved in my memory since Dr. Diallo wanted things to be clear between us from the first minute. In fact, Dr. Diallo did not even want an observation round.

I must admit that I did not expect this answer at all because I was spoiled in the past by having, as supervisors, people to whom I never cease, to this day, to pay tribute whenever the opportunity arises.

I was already starting to wonder what would happen next because threats in professional relationships, or any other relationship, have never been my cup of tea.

The representative wanted to make things clear from the commencement and I must admit that she could not be clearer than that. In this area she deserved a gold medal.

Although I was very surprised by Dr. Diallo's response, I tried not to take her reflection too seriously, but the future proved me wrong, and Dr. Diallo did not distinguish between herself and the institution she was supposed to serve. She had, in fact, always acted as if the WHO belonged to her and had always used the attributes of her position within WHO to settle scores with the employees.

Dr. Diallo seriously thought that was not accountable to anyone for the use of the WHO funds. She had always, during my time at WHO, acted as if WHO funds were her own. Indeed, she did not give a damn about the rules and regulations of the Organization in the management of WHO assets since she thinks that the rules and the regulations are the products of the white men.

Those are the reasons that permitted her to bring back with her from Luanda a young Angolan girl, aged 13, who was to serve as her slave. Yes, you read that right; I did write slave.

The WHO Regional Director for Africa, Dr. Luis Gomes Sambo, himself of Angolan nationality, was aware of this story, having met the young girl during his successive visits to Bamako and having been informed, naively, by me during a dinner I had with him during one of his business visits to Bamako.

Wanting to know how things were going in light of the fact that the WHO representative in Bamako and the administration officer, myself, were both new to the WHO office in Mali, I explained to him, in great details, that the problems in the WHO office in Bamako had nothing to do with the fact that we were new to our posts but would arise from the fact that the representative's behavior in the matter of the non-schooling of the 13-year-old girl she had brought back with her from Angola to look after her household was beginning to raise questions within the United Nations agencies, specifically within UNICEF.

In fact, during a discussion I had with them, the UNICEF officials did not mince their words in expressing their dismay that Dr. Diallo had caused them with her decision not to educate the little girl she had in her house and about whom they knew nothing. They explained to me that it was very difficult for them to promote the education of Malian children when a manager of a specialized UN agency refused to do so.

They did not hesitate for a second to describe as modern-day slavery the behavior of Dr. Diallo in the matter of the schooling of the little Angolan girl they called "Housemaid."

UNICEF staff members had shared with me their shame at finding themselves in situations where they had to explain the incomprehensible to their partners with whom they make considerable efforts daily to achieve the following five goals:

1. Survival and development for every child;
2. Education for every child;

3. Protection of every child from violence and exploitation;

4. A safe and clean-living environment for every child; and,

5. Equal opportunities for every child.

UNICEF employees had a hard time understanding the behavior of the head of a specialized United Nations agency, the WHO in this case, who meets on the third Thursday of each month with representatives of other United Nations agencies at the UNICEF office in Bamako to discuss the schooling of Malian children, who was herself against the schooling of an innocent girl whom she had uprooted at a very young age, in total contradiction with the speech she gives during those meetings.

Yes, there is an ocean of lies between what Dr. Diallo says in public and what she does in real life. She shamelessly said in one of the staff meetings that her dream is to build a school in Mali so poor children can go to school.

I later learned that Dr Sambo, WHO Regional Director, had turned a blind eye, or rather had chosen to turn a blind eye, in this matter because Dr. Diallo had him, literally and metaphorically, by the balls.

As I spoke to Dr Sambo about the Angolan girl's condition, with the hope of seeing her in school one day, I was far from suspecting that the WHO Regional Director for Africa was aware of the ins and outs of the little Angolan girl's story in minute detail. He knew this story because it was part of the story that led to Dr. Diallo's appointment as WHO representative in Bamako, which had begun nine years earlier in Harare, Zimbabwe.

I later concluded that when he was inquiring about the situation in the Bamako office, Dr. Sambo was not at all interested in knowing how things, for which I was responsible, were going. He wanted me

Modern Day Slavery

to give him the temperature of the pot. In other words, he wanted to know what I knew about the little Angolan girl and the representative's child.

Yes, three weeks before her arrival in Bamako, Dr. Diallo had sent a 10-year-old child to her friend, Dr. Soumare, so that he could go to his new school after the end-of-year holidays at the same time as all the other children. Dr. Diallo, who was due to return to her post on January 3, 2008, had delayed her arrival to Bamako so as not to do the handover with Dr Saar. This scheme allows her to avoid assuming the responsibilities that she did not want to assume under the pretext that she was not aware of them since she had not signed the handover.

Dr. Diallo had scrupulously kept me away from the girl and the boy who lived with her for reasons worthy of Alfred Hitchcock's thriller "Rear Window". When the dice fell, I learned that she had a thousand and one reasons for hiding what she was hiding from me. For my part, the personal affairs of the WHO representative in Mali were the least of my worries, as long as they did not involve WHO, given all the challenges that awaited the WHO representative office in Bamako.

We had, indeed, a very big challenge awaiting us in November 2008. Bamako was going to host the Global Ministerial Forum on Research for Health from the 17th to the 19th of November 2028. Bamako was expecting no less than 1,200 delegates for this forum who were going to join us from all four corners of the world. The WHO was a major stakeholder in this forum.

As if that was not enough, WHO was in the process of implementing one of the biggest administrative changes in its history, the introduction of GSM (Global Management System). The decision to introduce a modern management tool for the entire

Organization was taken at a high level in 2003. The objective of this decision is to improve the administrative and operational efficiency of WHO. It is the first effort to connect the Headquarter, the Regional Offices, and the Country Offices to a single management system.

This change would have a profound effect on the way the Organization did things.

It would dramatically reduce misappropriation of funds within the World health Organization.

No one shall be held in slavery or servitude:
Slavery and the slave trade
are prohibited in all their forms

- Article 4 of
the Universal Declaration of Human Rights

At the end of the month of June 2008, just when I thought I had put the issue of the little Angolan girl behind me telling it as it is to Dr. Diallo, I received a phone call from Mr. Gunther Baugh, administration officer of the WHO representation in Angola. A phone call that ruined the rest of my days in Bamako.

Baugh wanted to hear from the little Angolan girl who was with Dr. Diallo because her father could no longer contact her since the representative decided to stop answering his phone calls.

I didn't understand why Gunther was talking to me as if I was supposed to be in on what was going to be a big story. For his part, he was surprised to learn that I was completely out of the game.

The rest of the discussion allowed me to understand that the girl that Dr. Diallo had brought with her from Angola was the daughter of a driver at the WHO representation in Angola. The latter had lost his wife who had left him with five children. Dr. Diallo had taken advantage of the driver's misfortune by asking him to let her take care of one of his daughters.

Naively perhaps but certainly forced by fate, the driver accepted Dr. Diallo's proposal, thinking that at least one of his children would come out of the mud and secure her future. He probably never believed that one day he would not be able to speak to his minor daughter for more than two months.

This is the setting in which the approach of the administration officer of the WHO representation office in Angola took place. In clearer terms, he wanted to know if I could arrange a telephone conversation between the father and his daughter.

I literally answered him that:
Yes, there is a little girl who lives with the representative.
No, I don't know if she is the driver's daughter or not.

I also made it clear to him that there was no question of me arranging a secret telephone conversation between the daughter and her "father". All I could do was to bring to Dr. Diallo's attention the fact that the father wanted to speak to his daughter.

Grasping that he was unlikely to speak to his daughter anytime soon, the father wanted to, at least, know if she was schooled. My throat ached when I had to tell him that his daughter was not in school and that if the discussion, I had with Dr. Diallo, the previous month, was any indication, his daughter was not going to join the school benches anytime soon, if ever.

When I learned that the father wanted to know if his daughter was schooled, I couldn't help but think of my father, who died eight years earlier, who didn't have the chance to go to school but, with my mother, sacrificed themselves so that their ten children, five boys, and five girls, could go to school. My father always told me: "*My son, I am going to leave you something as a legacy that no one can take away from you: your education.*" Education was, indeed, sacred for my father.

That night, I could not close my eyes. I felt unfit because I did not have the courage to tell the father that his daughter was raped by one of the guards who was monitoring the residence of Dr. Diallo who, instead of filing a complaint with the police for rape of a minor, was negotiating with the security company SOGESBA on the back of his daughter.

The next day, as I was heading to work, I had only one thing on my mind: I wanted to burst this abscess that was growing because I didn't want to relive another night like the night before. To calm my mind, I meditated for a long time before leaving my house for work.

By keeping my promise to tell Dr. Diallo that the father wanted to speak to his daughter, I was very far from guessing that I had just signed the act of separation, or rather of divorce, with the World Health Organization.

Knowing my position on the issue of the girl's schooling, having discussed it with her a month earlier, Dr. Diallo took it very badly that I had told the "father" that his daughter was not in school. She expected, perhaps, that I would cover for her and would tell lies to the girl's "father," as she knows very well how to do.

What Dr. Diallo did not know, however, is that the art of lying is not within everyone's reach. She considered lying to be a natural act. Indeed, she convinced herself, over time, that lying is something congenital in human beings and not something a person acquires or reject according to the education they receive.

Our working relationship had taken a very bad blow since that day. That discussion had, in fact, signed the death certificate of our professional relationship. This relationship was not at its best before but it seemed to survive our differences regarding the application of WHO regulations. Regulations that were the work of the white men for Dr. Diallo who took every occasion to remind me of that.

Dr. Diallo had only one thing on her mind since that day; to put an end to any relationship I might have with the United Nations in general, and with the WHO in particular.

To achieve her goal, Dr. Diallo stopped at nothing. In addition to lying, for which she had a supernatural penchant, she added defamation, forgery and the use of forgery and the falsification of documents. Her cabal began a day after our conversation.

Since my early youth, I have always wanted to work for the United Nations or a specialized agency of the United Nations. My work at the American Friends Service Committee (www.afsc.org), a Quaker organization that works with communities around the world to combat injustice and create conditions for lasting peace, known for its commitment to nonviolence and its belief in the transformative power of love to overcome conflict and oppression, only strengthened this desire.

When the WHO Regional Office for Africa decided to offer me a temporary contract as an administration officer for their representation office in Bamako, I was over the moon not only because one of my dreams had come true but also because I was going to make this dream come true in my continent: Africa.

What I never suspected, when I went to Bamako on November 9, 2007 to fulfill my obligations, was that this dream would turn into a nightmare.

I spent two pleasant first months with Dr Lamine Cisse Saar as my superior. Two months during which I had savored every minute of my presence in the office. Dr Saar was always available to answer every and each professional question I had. At no time during these two months did he ask me to contravene a regulation of the organization for his personal benefit. On the contrary, he was always delighted to see me ensuring compliance with the rules and regulations.

Modern Day Slavery

I will never forget his reaction at the Bamako airport on Saturday when he was to leave Mali for Mauritania to take up the position of WHO representative in Nouakchott. Noticing that I had asked just the driver who had taken him to the airport to go home since his services were no longer needed, Dr Saar turned to the officials who were at the airport to thank him for his loyal services in Bamako and to wish him a safe journey, to ask them if they had noticed something. Since no one knew what Dr. Saar was referring to, he followed up with another question: *"Why did the administration officer ask only the driver to go home?"*

Seeing that nobody wanted to take the chance of answering his question, he explained to them that the driver was the only person who was paid that day. He was paid at the weekend rate. Mr. Benakezouh had released him because he was looking after the organization's funds. It was up to the driver to tell him that he wanted to stay until the end without being paid from now on if that was his wish.

Dr. Saar could not leave Bamako without asking me a question that was close to his heart. Just five minutes before the doors of his gate closed, he looked me in the eyes to ask me which wine I preferred: red or white? Without waiting a second, I answered him: it depends on the meat on the menu. Dr Saar could not hold back; he had shouted, I knew it, three times before leaving us.

I had never suspected at that time that I was living the end of a dream. The awakening on Thursday, January 24, 2008, was abrupt and brutal. I found myself, in fact, working with Dr. Diallo whose personality is diametrically opposed to that of Dr. Saar.

In deciding to join the WHO, I had never thought that I would be an accomplice to modern-day slavery and rape of minors.

I believe I did what I knew how to do in these cases. I reported everything I witnessed to all the people and all the authorities, and I continued to do so sixteen years later.

I will help my colleagues and their families in adversity

- The Hippocratic Oath

Having had excruciating lower back pain, my doctor suspected a kidney stone after telling him that I had had a kidney stone in the past, and the intensity of the pain was much the same.

Following my doctor's recommendation, the WHO had decided to evacuate me to Paris for treatment. To do this, I had to wait for the "travel authorization" from Brazzaville, where the WHO regional office for Africa is located.

Once prepared, the document should be sent by email to the representative who was supposed to bring it to me at the "Pasteur Clinic", a private clinic where I had to spend the night of Thursday waiting to receive my authorization to travel. I finally ended up spending four nights in the clinic, consuming morphine every four hours to alleviate unbearable pain.

On Friday, the WHO office in Bamako closes at noon. Around 4:00 pm, Dr. Diallo came to visit me at the clinic. Seeing the state I was in, she was "sorry" for the delay caused by the employees of the regional bureau. She swore to me that she had called Brazzaville to speed things up. She also told me that she had just checked her emails before leaving her office to come to see me and that there was nothing. She even swore in the name of God "Wellahi".

Unable to understand why Dr. Diallo had sworn in the name of God and bored to death at the clinic, I asked on Sunday morning for a permission to leave the clinic for two hours in order to see what I could do to obtain this authorization to travel as soon as possible.

I took a taxi and went to my office to check my emails. To my great surprise, I discovered that an email had been sent on Friday morning, at 10:31 exactly, to Dr. Diallo with, as an attachment, a copy of the travel authorization. I was copied in this email.

The email was as relieved as I was when I first laid eyes on it. I couldn't help it but have tears in my eyes when I saw a pdf copy of the travel authorization. I finally saw the light at the end of the tunnel.

I also learned, through my administrative assistant whom I caught in my office rummaging through my documents, that she was doing that at the request of the representative who was doing everything possible to have me temporary replaced during my absence.

In fact, I discovered later that Dr. Diallo asked the regional office to allow her to hire an interim administration officer for the five days I would be in Paris for my treatment. She wanted a replacement because she wanted to have a person, she trusted, who could have access to my documents during my absence to check for any damaging records I might have on her. And God only knows how many documents I did have.

Dr. Diallo lied to me on Friday, swearing in the name of God that she did not receive my authorization to travel because she was hoping to hire my replacement before I left for Paris. I will, therefore, hand over to them a copy of all the files I was working on.

The gesture made by my administrative assistant was not an isolated act. I had doubts that the representative had formed a team of 4 employees who were the only ones, among the 31 employees of the WHO representation in Mali, who had agreed to play her game. A game that consisted on building a wall between me and the employees in order to isolate me. These four employees had agreed to play the representative's game because each of them had a vulnerability on which Dr. Diallo could rely to make them sing *"God Save the Queen."* The queen is, of course, Dr. Diallo.

Even though I was very aware of the stabbing behind my back, I did not change one iota my conduct towards the national employees of the WHO representation in Bamako because I knew that the survival instinct pushed them to do things that they would never do in normal times and normal places.

Dr. Diallo knew that national employees were vulnerable and that her relation with them were essentially guided by this vulnerability. On the other hand, her behavior with the international employees, who were three in number, including myself, followed a different logic.

It was this vulnerability that had allowed her to recruit into her team of missionaries a doctor who was on probation, a driver who had been recruited on the basis of a falsified school certificate, another doctor whose contract was coming to an end and therefore subject to renewal, and my administrative assistance to which she had dangled the position of administration officer.

For the other officials who were less vulnerable, such as the librarian, Dr. Diallo had resorted to mission expenses (commonly called per diem) whose amounts were calculated on a daily basis and depended on location of the mission.

These amounts were considerable for national civil servants. A 4-day mission could bring in the equivalent of a month's salary for national civil servants. Dr. Diallo made excellent use of this allowance to try to obtain the support of civil servants in her conquests.

I am the first person to admit that I did not have a unanimous support among the employees of the WHO representative office in Mali and I had no interest in having that. My parents had always taught me that I should worry more when I have a unanimous consent than when I don't have it because you cannot please everyone in this world. And if you do, it is because you made a lot of concessions.

There were, in fact, four employees who, for reasons known to all other civil servants, did the dirty work of the representative in private. I will not dwell here on the behavior of these people because I have no intention of demeaning them in my book. Moreover, demeaning people is not in my genes and the importance of the book lies elsewhere.

With the travel authorization in hand, I returned to the hospital to spend my last night at the clinic and to pack my things for a Bamako-Paris trip scheduled for the next day at 9 pm.

Just as I was getting my thoughts in order, an elderly person came into my room. Having noticed my surprise, the person didn't give me time to question him before he started talking.

- *Are you the administration officer of the WHO?"*

Before answering his question, I wanted to know who I was dealing with.

- *I am Professor Mamadou Dembélé; I am the uncle of your secretary, Mrs. Aoua Dembélé.*
- *If I told you that I am the administration officer of the WHO, would you believe me?*
- *I just confirmed that you are the one I wanted to see. My niece told me about your sense of humor.*

- Yes, I am indeed the administration officer of the WHO, and my name is Nour-Eddine Benakezouh.

- I learned through my niece, who visited you yesterday, that your pain is excruciating. Have they diagnosed anything?

- Yes, I think it is a kidney stone.

- I also learned that you are going to be evacuated to Paris and that you are just waiting for authorization to travel for that. Do you know which hospital you will be in?

- Since I can't hide anything from you. I have to tell you that I received my authorization to travel today, and I am going to visit a friend who works in the medical field in Paris and who made an appointment for me. To be honest with you, I don't even know the name of the hospital. Knowing the French health system better than I do, I completely trust him.

- Would you be interested in being treated by Professor Bernard Debré?

I was starting to think it was a hidden camera prank. So, I decided to play along.

- Do you think Professor Debré would have time for me? He must be quite busy with the current situation. And how do you suggest that I get in touch with him?

- Don't worry, I'll take care of all that. I'll get in touch with him tonight, and you'll get a call from his secretary tomorrow morning to give you an appointment.

- Don't tell me that you manage his appointments too. Besides, you didn't ask me for my phone number, how will his secretary reach me?

Having suspected that I had doubts about his promises, Professor Dembélé took care to speak to me pleasantly.

- *No, I don't manage his appointments, but he is an old acquaintance of mine. I met him for the first time with his twin brother Jean-Louis when they were six years old, during the visits I paid to their late father, Michel Debré, Prime Minister of the Fifth Republic under Charles de Gaulle.*

    As for your phone number, my niece Aoua gave it to me in case I had to call you to find out how you are. But I finally decided to visit you in person rather than calling you.

Professor Bernard Debré told me exactly the same thing about the conditions in which he had known Professor Dembélé. I also learned while talking with Professor Debré that Professor Dembélé was also Prime Minister of Mali in the not-distant past.

This latest revelation only increased the respect I had for Professor Dembélé, who had not, at any time during our discussion, felt the need to tell me that he was Prime Minister of Mali, and the esteem I had for his niece Aoua, my secretary, who never mentioned to me, even after my return from Paris, that her uncle was Prime Minister of Mali. This earned her a box of chocolates.

To give her a taste of her own medicine, I had never told her, to this day, that I learned that her uncle was Prime Minister of Mali. She will probably find out now by reading the book.

The gesture of my secretary Aoua, speaking to her uncle in order for me to be treated by Professor Bernard Debré, deeply touched me in more than one way. It confirmed to me what I had always felt: There were employees who supported me in my attempts to put an end to injustice, embezzlement, falsification of documents, lying, sexual exploitation, and modern-day slavery.

This gesture by Aoua had prompted me to send an email to all WHO employees in the Bamako office before my departure for France. An email in which I apologized to each of them who had honestly felt any aversion from me.

I took the time to write them the following:

"In accepting the offer from the Regional Office to serve as administration officer of the WHO Representation Office in Mali, I had only one idea in mind: To give back to this continent a little of what it has given me. So, I came to Bamako to serve and not to serve myself. Every night, before going to bed, I asked myself a single question: What have I done today that could change the lives of Malians in the slightest? My love for my continent, despite what I am experiencing, has not changed one iota."

The officials' replies to my email had the same effect on my soul that morphine had on my pain. They served as solemn confirmations of what I had always suspected. They assured me that the employees were sorting things out and separating the wheat from the chaff.

Some officials, in addition to responding to me in writing, took the time and care to call me to wish me a speedy recovery and to tell me that they would pray for me. After all this support, I felt like I was growing wings. I no longer needed to take the Air France plane to get to Paris. I could fly with my own wings.

Arriving at Bamako airport on Monday, July 7, 2008, I decided to inform the Air France station manager that I had a kidney stone and that everything had been under control since that morning but that there was a chance that my pain would come back in the middle of the flight. I tried to reassure him by telling him that I had morphine on me in case my pain decides to undermine my morale which was at a good level.

Not wanting to take any risks, the station manager, after taking my details, was categorical. I could not take an Air France flight as long as I did not have a medical certificate signed by the Air France doctor in Bamako authorizing me to do so.

The first thing I did the next day was to call Professor Bernard Debré to tell him the bad news and to apologize for the fact that I was going to miss the appointment I had with him that same day.

I told him that I was going to go to the clinic of the Air France doctor to try to obtain the medical certificate that Air France station manager had requested and to call his secretary back to make another appointment.

After that call, I went to see the doctor who, after calling the Pasteur clinic where I was hospitalized for four nights, gave me the medical certificate required by Air France.

Once I had the medical certificate in hand, I called Professor Bernard Debré again, who had given me another appointment for Friday, July 11 at 10:00. He had taken care to apologize because his secretary was going to be on vacation. To which I had replied that it was him I was going to see, not his secretary. Professor Bernard Debré could not hold back; he burst out laughing.

As things were going very well this morning, I wanted to take advantage of my lucky star to make my reservation with Air France for Thursday, July 10. I ended my prolific day with a phone call to my superior to inform her that I had just made a reservation for Thursday, July 10, at 9:00 pm.

Faced with the failure of her attempt to convince the WHO general management to appoint a person to replace me for a period of five days, Dr. Diallo did not sit back and do nothing.

Very early in the morning of Thursday, July 10, the day of my trip to France for treatment, Dr. Diallo called me to ask me to come to her office at 10:00 for my annual assessment.

Out of the 365 days in a year, Dr. Diallo couldn't find a better day to assess me than the day of my medical evacuation to Paris after four nights of hospitalization at the Pasteur clinic in Bamako, where I was treated with morphine to alleviate unbearable pain.

You would have to be blind not to see that Dr. Diallo had no intention of evaluating me that day. She was unable to do so because she had an important meeting at 11:00 outside the WHO office. She therefore had to leave her office no later than 10:15.

So, the following question stood up:

- *Why did Dr. Diallo call me in at 8:00 am for my assessment which was supposed to take place at 10:00 am when I was on medical leave and I had to prepare for a 6-hour flight which was supposed to take place the same day?*

To ask the question is to answer it; Dr. Diallo had no intention of evaluating me that day. She claimed that she wanted to do so because she had heard of the responses I had received from employees to my email and because she was convinced that I would refuse meeting her, given the state of my health. She needed a justification for her unilateral "evaluation" that was not in accordance with WHO regulations.

Surprised by my presence in her office at 10 am as she had requested, Dr. Diallo spoke to me in generalities even when I reminded her that this was my first WHO evaluation and that I needed all her help because, in addition to this fact, I myself had officials to evaluate and I needed all the help I could get from her.

Not being prepared for all this, Dr. Diallo excused herself, saying that she could not give me more time because she had a meeting in forty minutes.

Before leaving her office, I informed her of my desire to return in the afternoon and of my availability until 6:00 pm since my flight was a night flight.

To my great surprise, Dr. Diallo, who had decided at 8:00 in the morning to assess me on the day of my medical evacuation to Paris, changed her mind two hours later to tell me:

- *We will see each other when you return from France. Your health comes first.*

All the attempts to harm me having failed, Dr. Diallo had no other choice than to resort to lies, falsification of documents, forgery and use of forgeries to achieve her objective; that of separating me from the WHO to do what he wanted with the little Angolan and the funds of the organization.

Dr. Diallo had a thing or two to teach Edward Bernays about manipulating public opinion. She would stop at nothing to achieve her goal.

1. Gaslighting is her favorite manipulation technique;
2. She denies having said or done something, even if you have irrefutable proof;
3. She changes the subject or questions her victim's memory to destabilize them; and worst of all
4. She tries to isolate the victim from their friends, colleagues or supporters to better control them.

Nothing can better explain Dr. Diallo's relationship with lying than the story that took place on Saturday, August 2, 2008, in Teriya

Bugu, a rural development center located approximately 250 km from Bamako, where she had decided to organize a retreat for employees of the WHO office in Bamako. The retreat took place from August 1st to August 3rd, 2008.

On the second day of the retreat, for a very bizarre reason, Dr. Diallo, a football fanatic and a fan of Hafia Football Club, a Guinean team, suddenly decided, during a morning coffee break, to talk about a football match between her favorite club, Hafia Football Club, and the Algerian team Mouloudia Club d'Alger in 1976 in the final of the African Cup of Champions Clubs.

The WHO representative in Bamako wanted, for a reason she has a patent for, to make the 30 WHO employees seated at a table drinking their coffee or tea believe that Hafia Foot Ball, after suffering a 3-0 defeat against Mouloudia Club d'Alger in the first leg, came back from behind in Conakry to win the African Cup of Champions Clubs on penalties (4-1).

Of all the football matches that Hafia Football Club had played and that Dr. Diallo could have chosen to praise her favorite team, she staked her entire reputation on a match that I attended at the July 5th Stadium on December 18, 1976. Although I am not an MCA supporter, I accompanied a friend, a Mouloudia fanatic, who had given me his father's ticket to see the historic match with him. His father, another Mouloudia fan, had decided at the last minute not to go to the stadium because he was convinced that his team was not going to recover, given the humiliating defeat (3-0) suffered by his team on December 5, 1976, in Conakry. Mouloudia finally achieved a resounding feat by overcoming the Guineans with a score of 3 to 0 and 4 penalties to 1.

Dr. Diallo reversed the roles by awarding the African Cup of Champions Clubs to her favorite club, Hafia Football Club, which, according to her, came from very far away by scoring three goals against Mouloudia and winning (4-1) on penalties.

As Dr. Diallo passionately told her story, the WHO employees had their eyes fixed on me. They knew that the representative was practicing her favorite sport: lying, and that her goal in telling this story was to provoke me in the hopes of seeing me react badly in front of 30 witnesses. What they did not know, however, was how I would react.

When she finished her story, Dr. Diallo looked at me as if to say: If you have something to say, speak now, or you must hold your peace forever.

I looked at Dr. Diallo innocently before telling her:

- *You will never guess what the press told us in Algeria. They told us that it was Mouloudia who had won the African Cup of Champions Clubs. The most unbelievable thing is the fact that the supporters who were at the July 5th stadium to watch the match, and of which I was one, believed the lie of the Algerian press. Algerians, to this day, believe that it was Mouloudia who had won the cup.*

Needless to say, the table was cleared in less than a minute; the WHO employees wanted nothing to do with the rest of the story.

Faced with this bitter failure that Dr. Diallo really did not expect, she realized that time was not on her side. There was a sensibilization workshop on the Global Management System (GSM) that was to take place in Gaborone, Botswana, from September 18 to 22, 2008, and which was to bring together the WHO regional director, WHO country representatives, and liaison officers; the director of program management, the director of the division of administration and finance, the director of the division of AIDS,

Modern Day Slavery

Tuberculosis and Malaria prevention and control and the administration officers of the country offices. Dr. Diallo knew that I was going to meet the administration officer of the WHO representation office in Angola and that I was going to learn things from him about the little Angolan girl.

Dr. Diallo would not want to hear of a meeting between me and the administration officer of the WHO representative office in Angola. She was going to do all the gymnastics she could to prevent me from going to Gaborone, Botswana.

*Upon being admitted to practice medicine,
I promise and swear to be faithful to
the laws of honor and probity.*

- The Hippocratic Oath

Dr. Diallo stopped at nothing to stop me from attending the Global System Management (GSM) Awareness Workshop because she knew I was going to discover things she did not want me to discover.

When her manipulations and provocations fell through, Dr. Diallo changed her tune by resorting to lies, defamation and falsification of documents under the stunned gaze of the regional director. It was only later that I understood why the WHO regional management, at first, and the general management, subsequently, had turned a blind eye to all this.

Indeed, after four emails to the WHO regional bureau in which she went out of her way to remove me from the list of people who were to participate in the Gaborone workshop, Dr. Diallo resigned herself to accepting the decision of the WHO regional director who had to intervene, in person by email, to confirm my participation in the workshop.

Seeing that Dr. Diallo was stubborn in excluding me for reasons that he could not publicly endorse because they contradicted all the workshop preparation documents that we had received from him, Dr Sambo took the trouble to respond personally on September 10th, 2008 to one of Dr Diallo's emails intended for the workshop organizers, whom she had seized for a fourth time to decide on a question that was not one.

Modern Day Slavery

Knowing the privileged relations that Dr. Diallo had with Dr. Sambo, the organizers of the Gaborone workshop did not want to take any risks when deciding whether to keep me or remove me from the list of participants. They preferred to pass the hot potato to the regional director.

Dr. Sambo finally decided that it was I, because of my position in the WHO Office in Mali, who should go to Botswana. He had no other choice because he could not go against his own writings where he was very clear about the participation of country office administration officers in the Gaborone workshop.

He wanted to clarify the reason for this by referring to the correspondence signed by himself and sent by his secretary to all WHO representatives.

Dr. Diallo responded to this email by doing what she does best: Not taking responsibility by blaming others for her masterpieces.

Her secretary had paid the price this time since Dr. Diallo had written in response to the email from the regional director the following, *"My secretary forgot to give me a copy of the correspondence."*

This is Dr. Diallo at her best. Everyone who had worked with her will recognize her signature, her poor secretary first.

To believe that Dr. Diallo was going to stop there is to not know her or to demonstrate a grotesque nativity of which the children who believe or want to believe in Santa Claus are the authors.

It didn't take long for Dr. Diallo to get back in the ring and go for broke this time. Dr. Diallo couldn't wait more than two days before getting back on stage.

On Friday, September 12th, 2008, the representative asked me to get ready to accompany her to the airport on Sunday, September 14th, 2008, because she had to leave Bamako at 1:45 p.m. for Gaborone to participate in the GSM awareness workshop.

Until then, there was nothing new since she had always insisted that I accompany her to the airport each time she left or returned to Bamako, even when it was a personal trip. Something that Dr. Saar, the former WHO Representative in Mali, had never asked me to do and that no representative of the other United Nations agencies in Mali asked their administration officers to do. In addition to accompanying her to the airport, I had to wait there until the plane took off.

Surprised by the fact that I had not questioned her decision to take up a day of my weekend and determined to push things to the end in the hope of seeing me react badly, the representative called me on Sunday, September 14 at 9:00 in the morning to ask me to come to her house to pick up her luggage to check it in.

Surprised by the tone of her inquiry, I told her that her driver always checked her luggage and representatives of other UN agencies checked their own luggage. I wanted to know what had changed and why WHO should be different from other agencies. Dr. Diallo had replied to me curtly:

- *From now on, you will be the one checking in my luggage. You need to read your job description."*

Not wanting to give the representative any opportunity, I answered her as calmly as possible:

- *This is a great idea; I do need to be aware of my rights and obligations within WHO. That is why I have been asking you repeatedly to give me a copy of my job description at WHO."*

Surprised by my answer, which she did not expect at all, she could not help but tell me:

- *It is a little too late for that."*

At that precise moment, I was certain that the representative was going to go all out to write the death certificate of my relationship with the WHO.

I still ended the discussion with her by trying to reassure her, saying:

- *Even if I had to check in your luggage, it is very early to do it. The flight is at 1:45 p.m. I will come at 12:00 p.m. to do all that.*

The representative was starting to lose her bearings because her provocations were not bearing fruit. She had called me back at 10:00 to ask me why I was not yet at her place.

I repeated to her:

- *Since the flight is at 13:45, the airport is 15 minutes from your residence, and the check-in counters only open an hour before the flight, that is to say, at 12:45, I will be at your place at 12:00.*

The representative did not want to understand or listen to anything. She insisted that I go to her place right away, which I did. I arrived at the airport at 10:40 and had to wait until 12:45, in temperatures of over 35 degrees Celsius in the shade, to be able to check in her luggage.

Dr. Diallo had called me back, once again, at 12:30. She was still at home. She wanted, supposedly, to find out how things were going. In reality, she had called, this time, for no other reason than to enjoy her work.

She was still dreaming that I would make a faux pas and do something regrettable that she would use against me to prevent me from joining her two days later in Gaborone.

Having learned to read Dr. Diallo, like one reads a newspaper, I had told her that the check-in counter was still closed. She then "apologized" because she thought the flight was at 12:45. I couldn't help but ask her, as nicely as possible, what she was still doing at home if she thought the flight was in 15 minutes.

Dr. Diallo's behavior in this episode was nothing but provocation. I reached the point where nothing surprised me about her, not even her childish behavior that I began, paradoxically, to find amusing to the extent that it reminded me of the discussions I had with my classmates in the courtyard of the Victor Hugo school when I was in the fifth and the sixth grade.

What I will never understand, however, is the fact that the World Health Organization called upon people like Dr. Diallo to take charge of the destiny of Africans in terms of public health, while I know many doctors who could have rendered enormous services to their continent in terms of health and to whom the WHO had never given the chance to do so.

The question I was asking myself at this stage of my life was:

- *Would my meeting with the administration officer of the WHO representation office in Angola allow me to have an answer to my concerns?*

The answer to this question would cost the WHO Regional Directorate for Africa more than US$25,000. That was a waste of US$25,000 because the WHO had not taken advantage of the knowledge, I had gained at the Gaborone workshop.

Modern Day Slavery

The Management decided not to renew my contract after paying for my participation in the Botswana workshop. Participation that cost them an arm and a leg.

The world will not be destroyed by those who do evil, but by those who watch them.

- Albert Einstein

I left Mali for Botswana on the afternoon of September 16, 2008. I was due to arrive in Gaborone a day later after an 8-hour stopover in Dakar and a 2-hour stopover in Johannesburg. I spent the days of 16 and 17 September apprehensively preparing for my meeting with Gunther, Administration officer of the WHO Representative Office in Angola.

I had no idea what I was going to learn from this encounter, but I was sure of one thing: I was going to lose my virginity to the information about the little Angolan girl.

When we landed in Gaborone, I was ready for anything. I had prepared myself very well psychologically. I had only one question left that I could not answer because it did not depend solely on me. Gunther had, in fact, a say in the conditions of our meeting. I still did not know, in fact, whether we were going to meet publicly or privately.

Upon arrival at the Gaborone Sun Hotel where we were to be staying and where the GSM awareness workshop was to take place and after dropping off my luggage in my room, I headed to the bar to get a much-needed coffee. Although I was exhausted, it was very early for me to go to bed. It was only 5:00 pm. The coffee should keep me awake for another 3 hours.

I still don't know if it was the coffee that had done its job well or it was the meeting, by pure chance, with Gunther, that had made me forget my fatigue. Let's say it was both so that there would be no jealousy.

My bed had to wait for me for more than expected. Once in my room, my bed did not recognize the person it had met five hours earlier because I had become five years younger and I was on fire after the conversation I just had with the administration officer of the World Health Organization representation office in Angola.

In addition to rejuvenating and revitalizing me, the discussion I had at the bar allowed me to go to bed less stupid and less naive. I had learned things that allowed me to confirm my beliefs and get rid of all the doubts about Dr. Diallo that had been haunting me for eight months.

I had confirmed the serious doubts I had about Dr. Diallo concerning the assets and funds of the World Health Organization. Dr. Diallo never made a distinction between herself and the Organization. She used the latter's funds as if they were her own. She didn't start that in Bamako. Gunther had confirmed to me that this behavior was not new to her. To authenticate this, he brought to my attention the fact that Dr. Diallo had not paid her rent for the last 6 months before leaving Luanda. The World Health Organization had to pay its six months' rent to the Ministry of Health, which was the owner of the house where Dr. Diallo had lived during her mandate in Angola.

As I wanted to be sure that I had heard what he had just told me, I asked him clearly the following question:

- *Did you just tell me that Dr Diallo fled Angola without paying 6 months' rent to the Angolan Ministry of Health?"*

His response was immediate and could not have been clearer:

- *I will not go so far as to say that she fled Angola, but I would say that she left the country, leaving the WHO with, among other things, a debt of six months of her own rent to the Ministry of Health."*

After a night where I had slept like a log, I woke up in the morning a little later than usual but with a thirst for life that I had only known once before: on Saturday, June 13th, 1987, my graduation day from Drexel University in Philadelphia.

That day, when I received my diploma, I felt, for the first time in my life, that only the sky was the limit. The graduation song, "**The Impossible Dream**," had a lot to do with the feeling that had inhabited me that day.

The discussion I had with Gunther, twenty-one years later, had exactly the same effect on me.

I was eager to see Gunther again. We had arranged to meet at 4:00 p.m., just after the meeting that the administration officers of the WHO representation offices in Africa were going to have with Mr. Sander E. Haarman, Director of Administration and Finance (DAF) of the WHO Regional Directorate in Africa.

My meeting with Gunther was delayed by an hour because Mr. Haarman insisted on seeing me in private after our meeting. He wanted to discuss the WHO rules and regulations with me. The DAF informed me that my superior, Dr. Diallo, had complained to him about my ignorance of WHO rules and regulations.

I wanted to know if she told him which regulation she was referring to.

He replied: *"She was not specific; she spoke in a general manner."*

To which I responded most prudently by telling him:

- *I am new to WHO, and there are certainly many things that I still have to learn, but in order to respond reasonably to your concerns, I must know which regulation she referred to.*

It is true that I did not have the same reading of WHO regulations as Dr. Diallo but this is not due to my lack of knowledge of these regulations but rather to the willful ignorance and non-compliance to these regulations by Dr. Diallo when they do not suit her.

I suggested that she contacts the regional office to iron out our differences each time she tried to force my hand to do something that I believed to be contrary to the letter and/or the spirit of a WHO regulations. Something she had always refused to do.

Mr. Haarman did not expect my answer at all. So, he wanted to know if there was a particular case that I could share with him. Since there were several and we did not have time to review them all, I suggested the last case we had to deal with. This case concerned the moving of Dr. Diallo's belongings from Luanda to Bamako.

When moving from one country to another, WHO international employees have the choice between taking a lump sum and handling their own move or having WHO handle the transport of their belongings.

Dr. Diallo had opted for the lump sum. She was, therefore, solely responsible for her move.

In August 2008, seven months after her arrival to Bamako, Dr. Diallo called me into her office to tell me that her belongings had arrived at the port of Conakry and that I should contact the administration officer of the WHO representation office in Conakry to coordinate their transport from Conakry to Bamako.

I asked Dr. Diallo to provide me with all the documents concerning the move that she had in her possession. I took the documents she handed me and went back to my office to see how I was going to organize this transport.

As I looked through the documents that Dr. Diallo had provided me, I was surprised to learn that Dr. Diallo had opted for the lump sum formula. She was, therefore, solely responsible for her move. WHO therefore had nothing to do with the move of her belongings. I therefore didn't have anything to do with moving her belongings.

I called Dr. Diallo right away to tell her about my discovery and to tell her that I was going to bring her the documents that she had given me a few minutes earlier.

I expected everything from the representative except the language she used when I returned to her office to give her the documents; Language unworthy of a head of a specialized agency of the United Nations:

- *Who do you think you are? Two administration officers, the one from Angola and the one from Guinea, who are older than you and who know the WHO regulations better than you, have found nothing to say, and you are trying to philosophize with me.*

   You are worse than the white man when you try to imitate him by your behavior".

Convinced that the representative knew very well what she was doing since, at no time during her monologue, did she ask me what regulation I had relied on to reach my conclusion, I answered her with an Olympian calm:

- *I am not responsible for what other WHO office administration officers, whom I do not know and with whom I have never discussed this subject, do or do not do. I cannot therefore speculate on what motivated the actions that these administration officers took in this matter.*

Since speculation is not my strong point, I am not going to take the risk of starting to do so today. I can, however, tell you about the WHO regulations that are at the origin of my conclusion if you give me the time and the opportunity to do so. I will do so with supporting documents."

Dr. Diallo's response was immediate:

- *It's not up to you to explain WHO regulations to me. You keep your explanations and documents to yourself."*

I replied:

- *Perfect, so we could contact the WHO regional office to level out our differences in interpreting the regulations.*

Needless to say, that Dr. Diallo refused my suggestion by concluding:

- *No, I don't need to do that. I'll handle the matter myself."*

Dr. Diallo did, in fact, handle the last leg of her move herself, except that she did not renounce the use of WHO funds and labor. She did, in fact, call on two WHO drivers and had my administrative assistance pay for the rental of the truck used in the move.

One of the two drivers had crossed the Mali-Guinee border to go to Conakry without a mission order and was driving very late at night, breaking all WHO regulations on the matter.

These drivers charged the WHO office in Bamako 67 hours of overtime each in August 2008 for the time spent moving the representative's belongings. The representative authorized the payment of these overtime hours.

To appreciate things at their true value, I wanted to know when the representative had first approached him to tell him about my "ignorance" of WHO regulations.

Mr. Haarman answered me that the representative had whispered a word to him the day before during the dinner he had had with some WHO representatives.

I was sure, was my reply. It was just after she saw me with the Administration officer of the WHO office in Angola. I wanted to know if he did not find it a little strange that the representative waited eight months to raise with him an issue as important and urgent as that of my ignorance of the organization's regulations when my main role within the organization is to ensure compliance with those regulations.

Not wanting to hear anything from me anymore, Mr. Haarman completely changed the subject of discussion. He wanted to know if I had children. When he learned that I had two, he wanted to know their ages. To this day, I still have in my wallet two photos of my children which I proudly took the time to show him.

Mr. Haarman ended the discussion by asking me to take care of my children. Naively, I thought it was very kind of him to care about my children.

This sentence began to resonate in my ears two months later when I understood why the director of administration and finance insisted on talking to me about my children and why he asked me to take care of them.

I left Mr. Haarman to go and meet Gunther who was waiting for me impatiently because he was dying to know why the DAF wanted to speak to me in private.

I negotiated my information with Gunther. We came to an agreement; For every story he told me, I would tell him one, and he should start.

At the end of our discussions Gunther came to the conclusion that he should speak to the DAF about Dr. Diallo's mission in Angola and the effect it had on the WHO representation office in Luanda. He was convinced that Dr. Diallo had not spared him by talking about him to Mr. Haarman.

Gunther had a thousand and one reasons to be worried. When I learned the reasons for his concerns, I could only encourage him to talk to the DAF. Before leaving Luanda, Dr. Diallo had asked Gunther to write a memo in which he was to congratulate her on her management of the funds of the WHO representation office in Angola. According to him, He categorically refused to do so since this was far from being the case.

The only question that remained as we parted was whether he would do it alone or ask me to be a witness to his meeting with Mr. Haarman.

Unlike me, Gunther was very careful in his approach. His life experiences were different from mine. Indeed, my time with the American Friends Service Committee (www.afsc.org), a Quaker organization with 100 years of experience in building peace in communities in the United States and around the world and a co-recipient of the 1947 Nobel Peace Prize, had a lasting effect on me.

Like the Quakers, I believe that every person has an inner light that guides them toward good. This belief has made me always interact with people with the intention of lighting this light.

Personal integrity and sincerity are fundamental principles for Quakers. These are unfortunately principles that are seriously lacking in Dr. Diallo, Mr. Haarman and Mr. Durao.

> ***To be willing to march into hell for a heavenly cause***
> ***And I know if I'll only be true to this glorious quest that my heart will be peaceful and calm when I am laid to rest***
>
> **- The Impossible Dream**

The next morning, at around 6:00, I heard a knock on my door. When I opened the door, I was surprised to see Mr. Haarman.

I was wondering what he could be doing in front of my door when he started talking:

- Good morning, Nour. Have you had your breakfast?
- Good morning, Mr. Haarman. No, I just woke up.
- Would you like to have it with me?
- Give me time to brush my teeth, and I'll be with you.
- See you at the restaurant in 15 minutes.

On the way to the restaurant, I wondered what story Mr. Haarman would tell me this time. I was convinced that he wanted to continue the story he had short-circuited the day before. I had prepared myself to tell him other stories if the urge suddenly took him. And God only knows that I had stories to tell him.

To my great surprise, once seated, Mr. Haarman began the discussion without any observation round. He had told me that Gunther had gone to see him the evening before to talk to him about the little Angolan girl and the embezzlement of funds from the WHO office in Luanda.

Seeing a surprise on my face, Mr. Haarman wanted to know why I looked surprised since Gunther had told him that he had discussed the matter with me.

- *No, I am not surprised by the content of your discussion. Gunther had indeed told me about it. I am surprised by the speed of his action. When we parted yesterday, he had not yet decided whether he was going to come see you alone or whether I was going to accompany him.*

- *Anyway, now that we're all aware, I was wondering if I could ask you to do me a favor. I would like you to keep me informed of the developments in the situation of this little Angolan girl, once you will return to Bamako.*

- *Don't worry, I will do it as a duty and not as a favor. But before that, there is one a more urgent thing that I believe you should know.*

- *Can I know what could be so urgent?*

I wanted Mr. Haarman to know what was going on because Dr. Diallo was very keen to get her counterfeit $100 bill back from the bank and I was worried that things were going to get ugly. WHO was therefore in danger of finding itself managing a situation that could get worse.

I had explained to the DAF that Dr. Diallo had given the day before to the bank, which had a branch inside the hotel, a counterfeit US$100 note to exchange for Botswana Pula. The banker had discovered that it was a counterfeit note and had therefore decided to keep it by putting a stamp on it.

I continued my story by telling him:

- *Dr. Diallo came to see me yesterday to ask me to go with her to the bank teller to tell her that it was me who had brought this note from the bank in Bamako. I explained to the representative that I had nothing to do with this note and that it was her driver who had suggested that she*

> exchanges the currency on the black market, where the exchange rate was better than the rate offered by the bank. I told Dr. Diallo that I did not understand why she persisted in wanting to get the $100 bill back. I explained to her that she could not do anything with the bill since the banker had put a bank stamp on the bill, thereby making it void and that she is lucky that the banker had not called the police, who had an office just a stone's throw from the bank."

Mr. Haarman did not seem at all interested in the story of the counterfeit bill. There was no surprise on his face; which confirmed to me that he knew much more about Dr. Diallo than he wanted me to believe.

I regretted having promised him a few minutes earlier to do him a favor by keeping him informed about the little Angolan girl.

What seemed to me as a duty fifteen minutes earlier seemed like a disgrace now. I wanted nothing to do with the game the DAF was playing. I felt unfit. I was eager to leave the table.

Mr. Haarman's attitude is much more worrying than anything else. I have never met a person, in my life, as indifferent as him. Although the image of the organization for which he was administratively and financially responsible was threatened, he did not feel the need to lift a finger. He preferred to change the subject of discussion.

When I returned to Mali, I learned that the representative insisted on getting her counterfeit $100 bill back because she wanted to give it to her driver so that he could go and change it in the black market with the traffickers who had given her the change. Even without the bill, she had, in fact, asked her driver to go to the traffickers to bring her another $100 bill from them.

> *And the world will be better for this*
> *That one man, scorned and covered with scars*
> *Still strove, with his last ounce of courage*
> *To reach the unreachable star!*
>
> **- The Impossible Dream**

I left Botswana, not knowing what to feel. I had discovered a country that had pleasantly surprised me in more ways than one. I think that other African countries had a thing or two to learn from Botswana. I also discovered people who had surprised me for different reasons.

I had left Botswana knowing that I was going to turn a page of my life. I knew full well that Dr. Diallo was never going to sit back and agree to give up her feudal practices within a specialized agency of the United Nations, which had allowed her to enrich herself illicitly.

Dr. Diallo once swore to me, when she was trying to convince me to play her game, that she had never spent a penny from her salary since she was first appointed WHO representative.

I also knew that Mr. Haarman was far from being the person I should count on to free the little Angolan girl or to protect the assets and funds of the WHO as he had wanted me to believe. Unfortunately, the future had proven me right.

I also left Botswana with more questions than answers regarding Mr. Haarman's position on the matter of the representative's behavior within the WHO. The doubts I had about the DAF were fueled by his non-response to the gesture made by Dr. Diallo the day before our return to Mali.

Dr. Diallo actually came to see me to ask me to accompany her to the supermarket to transport her personal purchases to Bamako. She had clearly threatened me when I had kindly explained to her that I was not her valet.

When I asked Mr. Haarman if being the representative's valet was part of the administration officer's job description, he didn't know what to say.

His silence was revealing of the protection the representative was enjoying within the organization. What I did not know for the next 5 weeks was the name of the person providing this protection and why this person was doing it.

As soon as we arrived to Bamako, Dr. Diallo began the last kilometer of her Marathon, which started on the first Monday of May, a day after workers day.

The representative had no time to waste; she had only four weeks to achieve her goal of ending my career with WHO since she was so keen to keep her slave and to use WHO funds as she saw fit and not according to the rules and regulations of the organization.

Wanting to put all the chances on her side to end my career at the United Nations, Dr. Diallo did not rest on her lies and half-truths; she resorted to falsifying documents in full view of everyone. I often found myself pinching my thigh in front of her actions to make sure that I was awake and that I was not dreaming.

On September 25th, 2008, the day after our return from Gaborone, Dr. Diallo sent me an email asking me:

- *Send me the summary of your mission report. The report should clearly highlight the important points to be taken from the workshop and the urgent/immediate actions to be taken by the office team".*

Modern Day Slavery

On September 29th, 2008, I sent an email containing my report to all officials, including the representative.

On October 2nd, 2008, the weekly staff meeting took place. I made my presentation, which saw a large participation of the staff, who asked me, as expected, for explanations of an unprecedented change that was going to be initiated in their organization.

This was, however, a radical change in the way WHO does things. It is the lack of questions from officials that should be of concern, not the other way around. Officials at the GSM awareness workshop in Gaborone, Botswana also had questions. I did not hear a single person say it was because of the presentations.

Instead of rejoicing at the participation of civil servants who had a clear interest in this major transformation that their organization was going to undergo and upset by the failure of her attempt to manipulate those civil servants, Dr. Diallo then asked me to say in detail what is expected from each civil servant in the WHO representation office in Bamako.

I reminded the representative that:

- *I did not prepare such a presentation. I prepared, as you requested, a report that clearly highlighted the important points to be taken from the workshop and the urgent/immediate actions to be taken by the office team, not by each official. The detailed presentation of the role of each official will be the conclusion of the work that awaits us and not the introduction to this work. This is why those responsible for the introduction of GSM have decided to delay the implementation date, which was November 1, 2008."*

After persisting that the date of the launch of the GSM was still November 1, 2008, she insisted that I prepare a detailed presentation of the role of each official for the following day (Friday, October 3, 2008).

Dr. Diallo's request meant one of two things:

1. The representative didn't know what she had asked me to prepare as a presentation. If she did, she would never have dared to ask for such presentation if she had the slightest scruples. The work she had asked me to do was going to take me at least six months of consultation with the officials concerned. Dr. Diallo wanted me to personally do a collective work of at least six months in six hours;

2. The representative's objective was completely different from that of preparing the officials of the WHO representation office in Mali for the introduction of GSM.

The respect I have for every human being obliges me to opt for the second option. The representative wanted to break the momentum and enthusiasm that the officials had shown by participating in the way they did to my presentation. The officials knew that GSM would considerably reduce the misappropriation of funds from their programs; an enthusiasm that Dr. Diallo did not share for obvious reasons. GSM would put a stop to her non-compliance with the organization's regulations since, with GSM, everything would be done in real-time under the eyes of all the people concerned throughout the world.

In order to buy the time I needed to get in touch with the WHO regional office to clarify matters with the relevant officials; I had told the representative that:

- *I could prepare such a presentation for Monday, October 6th, 2008."*

Dr. Diallo would not listen because the successful launch of GSM was the least of her concerns. Worse still, she did not want GSM to be a success because it would significantly reduce her shenanigans. It would make it difficult, if not impossible, for her to embezzle funds. She knew this very well, and so did the officials.

Dr. Diallo, like all the other officials, had received my report on Monday, September 29th, 2008, three days before the October 2nd, 2008 meeting. If the representative had any reservations about my report, she could have expressed them before the meeting and asked me to include in my presentation the elements that she wanted to see in my report.

Better still, the representative could have prepared a presentation along these lines. She had attended, as I had, the GSM Botswana awareness workshop. This would have allowed officials to benefit from two visions of things rather than one.

The representative had done none of these things. Because the participation of officials in the discussion following my presentation was prolific, she had ended the fruitful exchanges to raise an issue whose sole purpose was to try to humiliate me by asking me to make a presentation other than the one she had asked me to make one week earlier.

As usual, Mr. Abdoulaye Cisse, secretary of the October 2nd, 2008 meeting, sent us an email on Monday, October 6th, 2008, in which he attached a copy of the minutes of the October 2nd meeting. The minutes were very well received by all the officials, with the exception of the representative.

Between Monday, October 6th, and Tuesday, October 7th, Dr. Diallo had privately asked Mr. Abdoulaye Cisse to amend part of the report, in total violation of the rules of the WHO Representation Office in Mali in this matter.

The rules require that the person concerned by the part of the minutes to be corrected or clarified should request by email from the secretary of the meeting, copying all the other officials, to correct the elements of his own intervention. The secretary then makes the corrections and submits the amended version of the minutes to the officials, which will then be adopted at the next staff meeting.

This way of doing things was the norm well before my arrival to Bamako and continued to be so throughout my mandate at the WHO Representation office in Mali.

On Wednesday, October 8th, 2008, at 07:55, Mr. Abdoulaye Cisse sent an email to the representative, without copying the other officials, submitting to her "the amended version of the minutes of the staff meeting of Thursday, October 2, 2008."

Four hours later, at exactly 11:40, the representative sent an email to the staff informing them of the following: *"Our Thursday meeting is postponed to Monday."* No reason was given for the postponement of the meeting, and no reference was made to the amended minutes that Mr. Abdoulaye Cisse had sent her privately earlier.

On Sunday, October 12th, 2008, Mr. Abdoulaye Cisse, a librarian, was sent by the representative on a mission to Brazzaville to participate in the workshop for analyzing data from the global survey on smoking among young people, which was to be held between October 13th and October 17th, 2008.

Mr. Abdoulaye Cisse had no qualifications or experience to participate in this workshop. His position at WHO had nothing to do with smoking. He is not a doctor and was not even a smoker to be able to talk about his own experience with tobacco.

The email from Mrs. Koundi Albertine, Secretary of MINH-TOB of the regional office, is very clear as to the person who was to participate in this workshop.

I quote:

- *The national authorities of your accreditation country are requested to nominate the GYTS Research Coordinator to participate in this workshop."*

Dr. Diarra Nazoum is the GYTS Research Coordinator appointed by the Ministry of Health. He did not understand the designation of Mr. Abdoulaye Cisse to participate in this workshop. He contacted me by email to get explanations regarding the choice of Mr. Abdoulaye Cisse, who is a librarian and who has never worked on smoking in his life.

Dr. Diarra Nazoum wanted to know what to do with the report he had prepared following the research he had undertaken, which was funded by the Center for Disease Control and Prevention (CDC) in Atlanta. The Brazzaville workshop was supposed to be the culmination of the results of all the research on smoking that had been done throughout Africa.

Everyone knew that by sending Abdoulaye Cisse to attend a workshop for which he was not qualified, Dr Diallo wanted to kill two birds with one stone:

1. She wanted to pay Abdoulaye Cisse, with WHO funds, for the services he had rendered her by secretly amending the minutes of the October 2nd, 2008 staff meeting. By going

to Brazzaville, Abdoulaye Cisse would receive a per diem for the days he was present at the workshop. Per diems are very important for national employees. A 5-day mission can bring a national employee the equivalent of more than a month's salary;

2. There was absolutely no question of Abdoulaye attending the staff meeting where the minutes of the October 2nd, 2008 staff meeting which he had fraudulently amended at the request of the representative, were to be discussed. His presence at this meeting would expose all of Dr. Diallo's manipulations. As a result, Abdoulaye Cisse had to be as far away from Bamako as possible. Brazzaville came, once again, to rescue the representative.

On Monday, October 13th, 2008, at 8:34, one hour before the staff meeting, the representative decided to forward to the officials, without any comment, the amended version of the October 2nd minutes.

Less than 30 minutes later, at exactly 09:07, I responded to that email saying:

- *For the part concerning me, I find that the first version of the October 2nd, 2008 minutes of the meeting is more accurate. I do not find myself in the corrected version of the minutes."*

Half an hour later, Mrs. Yattabary Aminata, Dr. Diallo's secretary, sent us an email postponing the meeting scheduled for 10:00.

Five more minutes later, Ms. Yattabary Aminata sent us another email scheduling the meeting for 1:00 p.m. the same day.

The meeting ultimately did not take place for reasons that I am still unaware of. No explanation was provided. I do know, however, that the representative had called officials to take the temperature. She realized that the vast majority of the officials were of my opinion. The amendments were illegals and did not reflect the discussions that took place during the meeting on October 2, 2008. She had, therefore, decided to back down.

On October 16th, 2008, Mrs. Yattabary Aminata sent us an email informing us that: *"The staff meeting of today 16/10/2008 will be chaired by Dr. Ignace Ronse NHP at 9:00"* without any other explanation.

The staff meeting was held under the chairmanship of Dr. Ronse in the absence of the representative. The minutes of the meeting do not mention Dr. Diallo in any of the three sections (present, excused, and officials on mission).

The officials present were at a loss as to what to do with the amended minutes of the October 2nd meeting.

Dr Ronse's proposal was included in the minutes of the meeting, "Concerning the report, which had been the subject of email exchanges, Dr Ronse, Chairman of the Session, proposed that each official correct the part concerning him/her of the electronic version of the draft of the report proposed by the secretary before the final version in order to avoid possible errors of interpretation."

I must admit, once again, that Dr Ronse is much more diplomatic than I am. He always knew how to find the right words to relax the atmosphere and to obtain consensus and/or approval. It should also be noted that he had ten years of experience in the field of public health in Mali. He must have seen some green and unripe things during this period. Time has allowed him to learn how to water down his wine and how to accept things. In one word, he came to the conclusion that he had to accept things he couldn't change.

Dr. Diallo wanted to amend a part of the minutes that did not concern her in very dubious conditions, not to say something else. The representative's behavior in this matter is not an isolated act. Dr. Diallo has always done so that the minutes of the meetings reflect her vision of things and not that of the people present at the meeting. The most eloquent example is that of the minutes of the Retreat of the Office of the WHO Representation.

I SOLOMNLY PLEDGE
To consecrate my life in the service of humanity
- WMA Declaration of Geneva

All the officials knew that the representative was not going to stop there. By her nature, she could not tolerate around her a person who was going to ensure compliance with the regulations of an organization that she believed to be hers.

The following question was on the lips of all the officials: "What is the representative's next attempt?"

For my part, I no longer knew which saint to pray to. I learned during the weekend who was behind Dr. Diallo. I also learned why Dr. Diallo allowed herself to behave the way she did. I had to face the facts that I was indeed in Africa and that nothing should surprise me. As an African, I had changed with time and my experiences but my continent remained the same.

On Sunday, October 12th, 2008, while I was having breakfast, I received a call from a WHO official who was on a mission outside the country. He informed me that he would be back to Bamako at 2:00 p.m. He wanted to know if I was busy that afternoon.

Since this doctor was a good friend, I took the liberty of asking him why he wanted to know if I was free in the afternoon.

I asked him a question that he found very funny:

- *Is it because your wife doesn't want to pick you up at the airport?*
- *No, Nour, I have some information for you that will shock you,"*

was his whole response. He wouldn't add a word.

Knowing my friend's seriousness, I arrived at the airport at 1:00 pm with the hope of seeing his flight land earlier. I had to wait thirty minutes longer than expected for him to arrive.

Taking advantage of my thirst for his information, my friend negotiated the exchange of the latter for a café au lait and a croissant at the restaurant Le Relax.

I accepted his condition without any hesitation since I intended to invite him for dinner in the same place. Since a coffee and a croissant would cost me less than a dinner, I added a bottle of water to his proposal.

On our way to the restaurant, I learned that the 10-year-old child who lived with the representative was the illegitimate child of the WHO Regional Director. The child was, in fact, born of an adulterous relationship that Dr. Sambo had with a WHO official in Harare where he was a Program Management Director in the WHO Regional Directorate for Africa. The civil war in Congo-Brazzaville forced the Regional Directorate for Africa to relocate its headquarters from Brazzaville to Harare in 1997.

Dr. Diallo, who began her career at WHO in 1999 in Harare, had adopted Dr. Sambo's child. In return, Sambo had guaranteed her a career at WHO. Unable to be satisfied with the career she had been offered, Dr. Diallo took over the entire Organization, running things as she pleased, completely ignoring the rules and seizing the Organization's assets.

The payment for services rendered began with Portuguese lessons for 6 months in Lisbon, at the expense of the princess, which happens to be the WHO, in this case.

Dr. Diallo had to learn Portuguese, the official language of Angola, so that she could represent the WHO in Luanda. Dr. Diallo's appointment to Angola would allow Dr. Sambo's illegitimate child to learn the customs and traditions of his father's country.

Dr. Sambo wanted his son to learn the language and culture of his country: Angola. So, he offered Dr. Diallo the position of WHO representative in Angola in 2024 on a silver platter.

I say offered because Dr. Diallo, even if she had the necessary training that I had never had the opportunity to appreciate while working with her, did not have the necessary experience to take charge of the WHO representation office of a country whose health challenges are the most important in Africa after those of Nigeria.

The position of WHO Representative in Angola, before Dr. Diallo's appointment, had been occupied by people who had worked in other African countries before applying for a posting in Angola. Dr. Diallo, on the other hand, took her first steps as WHO Representative in Luanda.

Surprised by my silence, my friend tried to reassure me by telling me that he had this information from a very reliable source; a doctor who knows Dr. Diallo very well for having worked with her in Harare and who knows that the latter had not given birth to a child before 2004, the year in which their destinies separated. The child, who was 10 years old in 2008, could, therefore, not be her biological son.

The doctor knew who the adulterous father was but did not know who was the child's mother. All he knew was that his mother worked at WHO and that she had found herself alone in Harare following the WHO's total relocation from Brazzaville to Harare the day after the outbreak of civil war in Congo-Brazzaville.

I wanted to reassure my friend that my silence was not dictated, at all, by doubts in his story. I was silent because I did not know what to say or what to do in the face of this situation and not because I did not believe what he was telling me.

A secret for a secret, I told him what Dr. Diallo had said to me a few days earlier during the United Nations barbecue, which partly confirmed what he had just told me.

That day, Dr. Diallo came to see me to tell me that she was going to leave the place because her son was unhappy. I wanted to know if he was sick because I could not understand how a child could be unhappy among so many children who were having fun as if there were no tomorrow.

She answered me:

- *No, he's not sick; he keeps asking me why all the children have a father and not him.*

Not knowing what to say and certainly not wanting to continue a discussion for which I was not at all prepared, I answered:

- *Yes, I think it's the right thing to do. You have to save him from living this nightmare any longer. You have to take him somewhere where he can forget all this."*

The representative had left the premises secretly, without making the slightest noise. She certainly did not want to have to answer to the people who were certainly going to ask her why she was leaving the premises only thirty minutes after her arrival.

I felt my friend catching his breath now that he knew I didn't doubt his story.

Once he had caught his breath, he couldn't help but ask me the question that had been asking itself:

- *Nour, what are you going to do now that you know who is behind Dr. Diallo?*

Without taking a second to think because I was unable to do so, I answered him:

- *I will first digest everything I have just learned. I will then mix all the ingredients in my possession to see what I will obtain. In other words, I have no idea what I must, can or will do.*

After a hesitation that lasted an eternity, he continued:

- *Nour, I'm sorry for you, but I have to tell you that I think that you're in deep shit.*

Feeling like a prisoner who had just regained his freedom, I answered my friend with a tick-tack:

- *I'm going to use this shit to fertilize the plants. The only downside is that I won't be among you to see these plants grow. It's going to take time, and time is a commodity that is becoming increasingly scarce for me. My contract*

> *renewal is due at any moment and the representative was going to do everything in her power to ensure that my contract renewal will not happen. She has a head start on me and time is definitely on her side."*

Now that the die had been cast, I was dying to know what damage the representative was going to resort to following the lamentable failure of her attempt to falsify documents for which the WHO representative office in Bamako and the Ministry of Health of Mali had paid the price. Indeed, a year-long research project on smoking had fallen through.

No one shall be subjected to arbitrary or unlawful interference with his privacy, family, correspondence or home, nor to attacks on his honor and reputation.

> - Article 17 International Covenant on
> Civil and Political Rights
> United Nations General Assembly
> 16 December 1966

On Thursday, October 2nd, 2008, the representative sent an email to all officials with the subject line: PMDS review. In her email, Dr. Diallo described the premises as related to her assessment of the officials.

At no point in her email did the representative allude to my refusal to be assessed. On the contrary, she stated in the same email that I was on the list of officials she had already met.

On Monday, October 6th, 2008, after a radio silence of almost three months (July 10th to October 6th, 2008), Dr. Diallo sent me an email informing me that she expected my documents no later than the following day, namely Tuesday, October 7th, 2008 before noon.

I reported to the representative's office four times on the day she had unilaterally set for my assessment.

I had the opportunity to be received by her very early in the morning (07:30). I explained to her that part A (Activity Plan) of my PMDS was ready but that I could not access it because of the problem we had with the computer network.

Dr. Diallo was sad to learn that my documents were ready but was happy to know that a problem with the computer network prevented me from having access and, therefore, from printing my documents. She had asked me to do it during the day.

Half an hour later, I learned that the computer network hadn't accidentally crashed. It didn't take a genius to figure that out when the IT officer called me to tell me he had a fever and couldn't come to work.

Faced with this situation that I did not find amusing at all; I did everything I could to get the computer network repaired. I called all the administration officers of the United Nations agencies to see if anyone of them could send us an IT specialist to help us out. The UNDP Deputy Resident Coordinator and Chief of Operations did not hesitate for a second to come to our aid. In addition, he made it his duty to give a ride himself to a UNDP IT specialist because there was no UNDP driver on site.

Once the computer network was repaired, around 10:00, I printed a copy of Part A of my PMDS and went with my documents twice, during the same morning, to the office of the representative who was, according to her, held by other obligations.

I had asked Mrs. Aoua Dembélé, my secretary, who was acting as the representative's secretary, to let me know as soon as Dr. Diallo had a minute to see me.

Having received no sign from my secretary, I went, at the end of the working day, for a fourth time, to the representative's office. Mrs. Dembélé, after consulting with Dr. Diallo, came back to see me to tell me that the latter asked me to come back the next day, although:

> 1. In her email the day before she clearly said that she expected the documents on Tuesday before 12:00; and

2. On Wednesday 8th and Thursday 9th of October, I had to go, as well as the representative and a large part of the officials of the Office to the global meeting Task Force of the UNDAF (WHO being the leader that year) which was held for two whole days outside of our office.

The high importance of this meeting was underlined by the representative in her October 7th and October 8th, 2008 emails addressed to all officials.

Dr. Diallo had even postponed the staff meeting from Thursday, October 9th to Monday, October 13th, given the importance of the UNDAF Global Task Force.

This maneuver has raised doubts about the objective of the Monday, October 6th, 2008 memo. Unfortunately, I did not have to wait long to see my doubts materialize.

Indeed, on Friday, October 10th, 2008 at 2:02 p.m. (the WHO office in Mali closes at 12:00 p.m. on Fridays and the organizing committee of the Bamako Forum of which I was a member meets at 3:00 p.m. every Friday), the representative had sent an email to Mr. Sander E. Haarman, DAF, with copies to Mr. Durao, Mr. Wadda and myself, telling him that I was unable to send her my PMDS and that she was going to send him her evaluation unilaterally.

Before Dr. Diallo sent her email to Mr. Haarman, her secretary called me to see if I was in my office. I told her that I was at the Ministry of Health for the weekly meeting of the Bamako forum organizing committee. The secretary wanted to know if I had access to my email. Since I had confirmed that I did not have access since I was out of my office, the way was clear for Dr. Diallo to send her email. She was reassured that I would not send my response until Monday, when I returned to work.

Modern Day Slavery

On Monday, October 13th, 2008, as soon as I became aware of the Friday, October 10th memo, I sent an email to Mr. Haarman and Dr. Diallo, with copies to Mr. Alvaro Durao and Mr. Alieu Wadda, disagreeing with the representative's assertions and expressing my willingness to be evaluated because:

> *One of my tasks within the WHO Representation Office in Mali is to ensure compliance with the rules and regulations of the organization. The PMDS being an integral part of these regulations, I am aware that I must, therefore, set an example in this area, especially since the process provides for a system of appeal if I were to question the objectivity of my evaluation."*

Dr. Diallo has, once again, completely ignored the fact that I had assured her in writing on October 13th that my PMDS was ready, that I was ready to be assessed and that I had attended her office four times on October 7th for my assessment. She preferred to send an email on October 14th to Mr. Haarman and Mr. Durao, with copies to Wadda and myself, including, as an attachment, her arbitrary "assessment" report.

The following questions arose when reading the representative's emails regarding my assessment:

1. What happened over the weekend between Thursday, October 2, 2008 -12:22 and Monday, October 6 -05:30 to justify the change in tone in the representative's emails?

2. When did she make the reminders, she refers to in her email of October 6, 2008? On Thursday, October 2, 2008, at 12:22, there was no mention of these reminders. The WHO office closed at 16:30 on Thursday, October 2, and at 12:30 on Friday, October 3; that gives 8 hours of work

between the email of Thursday, October 2, and the one of Monday, October 6, at 05:30 in the morning.

3. How could I refuse to be assessed on October 7, 2008, if I had seen no objection to being assessed on July 10, 2008, the day of my medical evacuation to Paris after a 6-day hospitalization in Bamako, where I was treated with morphine to alleviate excruciating pain? I had a very valid reason to refuse the assessment on July 10, 2008, given my deplorable state of health that day, and I did not do it because:

   a. I was keener than anyone to be evaluated since this was my first evaluation at the WHO;

   b. I had officials to evaluate, and I wanted the process of my evaluation to serve as a reference; and

   c. I was looking forward to this evaluation to clarify many things with the representative, develop my activity plan, and try to put an end to the moral harassment I was subjected to by the representative.

Dr. Diallo was very aware of all this and did not want this assessment to take place and did everything to do so, even depriving me of my most basic rights, namely the right to:

- Develop my work plan;
- Know exactly what Dr. Diallo was accusing me of;
- Have access to documents incriminating me; and
- Respond to the accusations made against me.

The Personnel Management and Development System (PMDS) is a three-step process:

   Step 1: Establishment of activity plans based on individual objectives;

Step 2: Ongoing feedback and dialogue on services, including a formal mid-term review;

Step 3: Year-end service review.

Dr. Diallo had not done the first two steps despite several requests from me. I had met the representative only once on this subject: on July 10th, 2008, the day of my medical evacuation to Paris, to develop the activity plan that was to be developed by January 2008 at the latest. Our meeting lasted less than 10 minutes, the time to present to the representative what I considered to be my objectives. Dr. Diallo then asked me to make them SMART without any further explanation, even though I was new to WHO.

Since there had been no activity plan, there had obviously been no formal mid-term review. Aware of these shortcomings in the procedure to be followed in terms of staff evaluation in accordance with Service Note 2001/37 detailing the procedure to be followed to implement the personnel management and development system, Dr. Diallo had done everything to ensure that stage 3 did not take place, going so far as to state that I did not want to be evaluated.

Dr. Diallo had, therefore, preferred to make a unilateral "evaluation" so as not to comply, once again, with WHO regulations and to give free rein to what she does best, namely lying, defaming, slandering, and falsifying documents.

Even by opting for a unilateral "evaluation," Dr. Diallo had refused to make available to me the annexes that she decided to send to Mr. Haarman, despite my October 15th and October 18th, 2008 emails. It was necessary to wait for the latter's intervention on October 27th for the representative to decide to make available to me only part of these annexes.

It would have taken 5 more emails (November 5th and 13th, 2008, and December 15th and 18th, 2008, and January 26th, 2009) and a wait of more than 3 months (October 14th, 2008, to January 29th, 2009) to receive the entire file of my "evaluation" from the regional office and not from Dr. Diallo whose behavior in this file can only be described as an abuse of power. The representative knew that she benefited from reinforced concrete protection. This allowed her to send packing everyone from the WHO regional office.

To obtain all the documents sent by the representative as annexes to her assessment, I had to raise my voice with Mr. Durao. The email I sent him on January 26th, 2009, is my best witness:

Dear Mr. Durao,

Despite your 15-12-2008 email in which you stated your availability to respond to my concerns regarding the non-renewal of my contract, my15 12-2008 and 18 01 -2009 emails have remained unanswered by you.

As I mentioned to you in my 13-12-2008 email, I intend to do everything humanly possible to set the record straight and to maintain my reputation and dignity that I have spent so many years building.

The false accusations of the WHO Representative in Mali and the falsification of the documents she sent you are quite serious matters in my book, and I am still convinced that they are also serious in the books of the World Health Organization. This is why I asked you in my 18-01-2009 email to kindly send me a copy of all the documents concerning me that were given to you by the representative who, despite the intervention of Mr. Sander E. Haarman asking her to give me a copy of these documents as soon as possible in accordance with the regulations and practices in this type of situation, only made part of the documents in question available to me.

I am merely communicating with you personally because I am convinced that it is in my interest, as well as that of WHO, to seek the truth in this unfortunate episode. If, for some reason, this conviction is no longer there, I will have no choice but to hand over the entire file to my lawyers.

Distinguished greetings

If the representative's behavior did not surprise me at all, having known her and worked with her for almost 10 months, I still could not understand the conduct of the regional office, and at its head Mr. Haarman who, although knowing very well the actions of Dr. Diallo in Angola, did not dare once, remind her of her obligations in terms of staff evaluation and respect for human rights.

Time had taught me that Mr. Haarman had decided to take Dr. Diallo's defamation and slander at face value, not because he believed her but because the decision not to renew my contract was made before receiving her evaluation. The latter was not the origin of the decision not to renew my contract but rather served as support for the decision that had already been made. This is why the regional management had deprived me of the right to reply, which is nevertheless guaranteed to me by the regulations of the World Health Organization that the representative accuses me of not knowing in her "evaluation."

The attitude of Mr. Haarman and Mr. Durao in this matter are no less than that of Dr. Diallo. Their comportment is unworthy of officials of the United Nations, whose General Assembly adopted on December 16th, 1966, the International Covenant on Civil and Political Rights, which clearly states in Article 17:

1. No one shall be subjected to arbitrary or unlawful interference with his privacy, family, home, or correspondence, nor to unlawful attacks on his honor and reputation.

2. Everyone has the right to the protection of the law against such interference or attacks.

The representative had set fire to the shack and the DAF did nothing to put it out or prevent it from spreading. Mr. Haarman had known since at least September 17th, 2008 what Dr. Diallo was up to. He also knew that she had sent him false documents and he had irrefutable proof that Dr. Diallo had herself falsified some of the documents she had sent him.

Although the matter is very serious, the DAF had not, at any time, felt the need to raise this issue with Dr. Diallo, especially when we know that Mr. Haarman was acting on behalf of a specialized agency of the United Nations, an international organization one of whose objectives, as described in its charter, is the protection of human rights.

Dr. Diallo had flouted all my rights under the approving gaze of the Director of Administration and Finance. All this was happening, believe it or not, within a specialized agency of the United Nations.

The speed with which my successor was appointed (less than a month), when we know that the position of administration officer had been vacant for almost two years before my appointment, has erased any doubt I may have had concerning the reason for the non-renewal of my contract.

The general management decided not to renew my contract at such a dizzying speed that they made more than one mistake:

1. The WHO Directorate General for Africa had decided not to renew my contract even though they had sent me to participate in the awareness workshop on the introduction of GSM in Africa, the most important change in the history of WHO.

2. My participation in this workshop took place 13 days before the date on which the WHO was to decide on the renewal of my contract and had cost the WHO representation in Bamako more than US$25,000, at a time when we had no funds for urgent renovations of our buildings, to comply with the recommendations contained in the "WHO Mali security plan, May 2008", prepared by Mr. Bertin Achidi, security officer at UNDSS. Because of its specificity to the WHO, my participation in the workshop could not be of use to me anywhere else. This is indeed a pure waste of funds on the part of the WHO.

3. The decision not to renew my contract was sent initially by email to the WHO representative in Burkina Faso. I had nothing to do whatsoever with the WHO representation in Burkina Faso. I was based in Mali and, to this day, I have never set foot in Burkina Faso.

4. In the same email, Mr. Durao from the WHO Regional Directorate for Africa wished me a happy retirement even though I was far from retirement age, and that was not the reason for the non-renewal of my contract.

The haste with which the officials of the regional management were forced to communicate to me a decision, which they all knew to be arbitrary and in contravention of all WHO regulations on personnel management and which was not taken by them, meant that they did not know which way to turn. I am convinced that some mistakes were deliberately made to ensure their protection in case things went wrong.

The behavior of the WHO regional management in this matter had only one objective: to protect Dr Sambo. The protection of Dr. Diallo was done consequently because she held the WHO regional director by the balls.

The regional management had been the subject of a concomitant sale: to protect the regional director, they had no choice but to protect the representative.

Like all sales, this sale had a price tag on it. It was the little Angolan girl, the modern-day slave, Mr. Nour-Eddine Benakezouh, the administration officer, and the WHO programs in Mali who were going to pay that price.

Indeed, with my departure, Dr. Diallo would keep her "modern-day slave" and would be able to dispose of the WHO's assets and funds as she wished without having to respect the rules and regulations of the organization and without having to be accountable to anyone.

> *Real obscurantism is not to hinder the spread*
> *of what is true, clear, and useful,*
> *but to bring into vogue what is false.*
>
> — Johann Wolfgang von Goethe

Unable to find valid reasons to question my work at the WHO Representation Office in Mali, especially when she saw that the employees were beginning to ask serious questions in staff meetings about the representative's relentless harassment of me, Dr. Diallo needed a document from another source to support her evaluation of me. The employees were her preferred source to give credibility to her assertions of "my incompetence, my poor ability to produce reports and summaries, my technical, managerial and behavioral weaknesses and my inability to complete the introduction of GSM."

Since she had not been able to have the October 2nd, 2008 staff meeting minutes, which she had unlawfully modified, adopted, Dr. Diallo had no qualms about submitting these minutes as if they were adopted by the staff. She knew that she was not risking anything by doing so because the WHO regional management was in her pocket. She, therefore, did send them documents to justify a decision already taken, that of not renewing my contract, rather than to allow them to arrive at the decision to renew or not to renew my contract.

Dr. Diallo did not stop there; she had the nerve to accuse me, in her evaluation of my work, of delaying the payment of WHO suppliers in a case that incriminates her personally.

She went so far as to submit invoices from SOGESBA, the company that provided security services for her residence, as proof of my delays in paying suppliers. In healthy organizations, you have to be sick to do something like that. Dr. Diallo knew that what she was doing wasn't logical, but she did it anyway because she had the balls in her hands.

Dr. Diallo, once again, submitted documents and made accusations without taking the time to explain things because these things legally incriminate her. I weigh my words very carefully when I say this.

The representative submitted the invoices for February, March, and April 2008 to me with a handwritten note: "AO + AA + FSO/Coulibaly. We must meet with this company before payment."

I had reassured the representative that I was not going to pay the bills for the simple reason that the AFRO-MEMORANDUM of BFO/AFRO of April 3rd, 2007, does not speak of payment of bills but rather of reimbursement of expenses upon presentation of the paid bill and receipts. In other words, the representative had to pay the bill for the surveillance costs of her home before requesting reimbursement from the WHO by presenting the paid invoice and the payment receipt.

WHO had no contract with SOGESBA to guard the representative's house. Therefore, it had no payment to make to SOGESBA. I made sure to give a copy of the memo to the representative.

The AFRO-MEMORANDUM of BFO/AFRO of April 3rd, 2007, was motivated by the concern of avoiding WHO paying the same security costs twice: once to the company that provided the security and once to the official who benefits from the security.

Dr. Diallo's goal in asking me to pay SOGESBA directly is to thwart the protective measure adopted by WHO. By forcing my hand to pay SOGESBA, she would be able to request reimbursement of these costs from WHO at a later date. The Organization will, as a result, pay twice for the same thing.

Dr. Diallo had done exactly that with the cost of moving her belongings from Luanda to Bamako. She had initially opted for the lump sum. Once the lump sum had been collected, she used the services of WHO to transport her belongings. By doing so, the representative had her cake and ate it too.

At the end of May 2008, Mrs. Yattabary Aminata, secretary of the representative, spoke to me about the payment of SOGESBA invoices.

I explained to her, in very clear terms:

- *"I cannot pay SOGESBA's bills for the simple reason that WHO had no contract with SOGESBA. I can reimburse the representative, as I do for other international civil servants (Dr. Ronse, Dr. Ndoutabe, and myself), but I cannot pay SOGESBA directly.*

    WHO has a contract with SOGESBA for the security of the WHO office. SOGESBA has been paid every month under this contract.

    If the representative wants me to pay the bills all what she has to do is to notify me in writing. That way, she will not be able to blame me for my lack of knowledge of the procedures and regulations."

I explained to the representative's secretary that the problem her superior had with SOGESBA should be resolved by the police and not by me. That is why I refused to meet SOGESBA officials, as the representative asked me to do in this case.

Mrs. Yattabary was not surprised to hear me talk about the police because she understood that I knew why the representative wanted to meet with SOGESBA officials.

To put an end to this game, which I really did not like, I explained clearly to Mrs. Yattabary what I thought of this case. I told her, among other things:

- *"Dr. Diallo must go to the police to inform them that the little Angolan girl was raped by one of the guards who was watching her house. She should not meet with SOGESBA officials, under any circumstance, to negotiate with them on the back of the little Angolan girl.*

  Rape of a minor girl is a crime and should be treated as such. I met Dr. Diallo and explained to her exactly what I think. She knows all this very well. I wonder why she keeps asking you to contact me for a case that is not of my responsibility."

Surprised by my reaction because she had never seen me in this state, I explained to her that rape of a minor is a very serious thing in my book, and that is what explains my reaction.

Although the April 3rd, 2007 memo was very clear, I sought clarification from Mr. Jules Bekombo of the regional office, who confirmed my interpretation of the memo, and who sent me another email dated June 6th, 2008, with an attached AFRO-MEMORANDUM dated June 5th, 2008.

Against all expectations, the representative sent me a mail processing sheet on September 29th, 2008, on which she had written the following note:

- *"AO, I do not understand why the agency has not yet been paid when everything is in... My security depends*

> on it. *I am not satisfied with your way of handling files with service providers who always complain about the slowness of payment when the funds are available. Also, this is the source of the low level of budget consumption when we are up to date in the implementation of activities. You are therefore responsible for this... from AFRO and the RD."*

It is very important to note that the representative knew very well what she was doing when she sent me this note. That is why she never finishes compromising sentences. She prefers to use suspension points in these cases.

I have only applied the directives contained in the April 3rd, 2007, and June 5th, 2008 memos which authorize reimbursement upon presentation of documents (paid receipt and invoice).

I have found myself in unenviable situations on several occasions when the representative's requests were so non-compliant with the regulations and procedures that I wondered whether she wasn't testing my knowledge of the regulations. The case of payment of invoices for security services went a little further because SOGESBA did not give in to the blackmail that the representative wanted to exert on them.

I wonder, to this day, how the representative could have thought for a second that I was going to negotiate for her the rape of a minor. Yes, Dr. Diallo, instead of filing a complaint with the police for the rape of a minor whom she was using as a slave, spent 5 months negotiating with the SOGESBA company with the hope of not paying her bills. In addition to not paying her guarding bills, Dr. Diallo wanted SOGESBA to give her a receipt for payment. That way, she could get reimbursed by the WHO for the guarding fees she had not paid.

Dr. Diallo had finished her "evaluation" by accusing me of the following:

- *"The administration officer caused considerable loss of funds for ongoing activities and delays in the implementation of work plan activities, resulting in a certain loss of credibility of the office with the Ministry of Health and suppliers, and led to conflicts that damaged team spirit within the office."*

Dr. Diallo has shown herself, once again, to be stingy with explanations. Trying to ask her for details about her accusations is a waste of time. The time and energy invested in this will not lead to anything concrete. The best dentist in the world will not be able to extract explanations from her.

It is a defense mechanism that she has developed very well and which has allowed her, among other things, to hide her deficiencies and her schemes.

To understand Dr. Diallo, we must, therefore, proceed differently by asking the right questions:

1. Why does Dr. Diallo never provide supporting evidence for her accusations?
2. Why does Dr. Diallo always talk in generalities; she never focuses on specifics?
3. Why does Dr. Diallo never raise the problem in time and place?

The answer to these questions is very simple: As a football fanatic, Dr. Diallo knows that the best way to defend yourself is to attack. With this maxim, she has lived her life blaming others for her own behavior.

Since Dr. Diallo has once again been stingy in her comments, I will provide some details regarding her false accusations.

Yes, the WHO representation office in Bamako was experiencing delays in implementing the activities of the work plan signed before Dr. Diallo's arrival to Bamako.

No, I was not the cause of these delays. Dr. Diallo, by not respecting the letter and spirit of the work plan signed by the WHO and the Ministry of Health of Mali, which is at the origin of these delays.

I have repeatedly found myself in situations where I was forced not to give my approval for the execution of an activity because it was not mentioned in the Work Plan. One of my tasks within the WHO Representation Office in Bamako was to scrupulously ensure compliance with the content of the Work Plan before approving any activity.

The representative could insist after my refusal to approve an activity, but she had to do it in writing to avoid any confusion.

Very aware that some of the activities she wanted to carry out did not comply with the regulations, the representative used other officials as a buffer zone to obtain approval for activities not included in the work plan.

To better understand certain things, I will give the best example to explain how the representative proceeds to have an activity approved even if the activity was not scheduled in the work plan.

Wanting to impress the delegates who were to travel to Bamako from November 16th to November 20th, 2008, for the Global Ministerial Forum on Research for Health, the representative decided to change the car of the WHO representation office, which was in good condition, for a Mercedes-Benz S-Class.

Surprised to learn that Dr. Diallo wanted to buy this vehicle, I informed her that this purchase was not in the budget of the WHO representation in Mali, which did not have the means to afford such a vehicle during this period.

The representative sought the necessary funds for the purchase of this vehicle from the budgets of Dr. ... programs; a perfect example of embezzlement.

When the representative insisted on buying the Mercedes-Benz S-Class, I informed her that no other UN agency, including UNDP, had a MERCEDES S 500 in its fleet and that the only person who drives a MERCEDES S 500 in Bamako is the Prime Minister of Mali. That Mercedes was a gift from the German government. I advised Dr. Diallo to think about what would be said in other UN agencies, in the Ministry of Health, among WHO partners in Bamako, and the organizations that we were soliciting locally to fund our programs.

To my great surprise, Dr. Diallo answered me curtly:

"It's their problem, not mine."

Faced with the representative's persistence in diverting funds from a program to be able to ride a Mercedes-S Class, I had no choice but to wash my hands of the matter by bringing the representative's intention to the attention of the regional office.

To my great surprise, the regional office did not object to the representative's idea of buying a Mercedes with funds from another program. They simply softened the representative's wishes by allowing her to buy a Mercedes E-Class. The poor representative should settle for that instead of a Mercedes S-Class. Life is unfair.

Dr. Diallo, the person who embezzled WHO funds, takes the liberty of contacting Mr. Haarman, the person who authorized this embezzlement, to accuse me of "causing considerable funds to be lost for activities currently being implemented and delays in the implementation of work plan activities, resulting in a certain loss of credibility of the office with the Ministry of Health and suppliers, and leading to conflicts that undermined team spirit within the office."

Walt Disney, creator of Mickey Mouse, would not have thought of such a scenario. He had to team up with Aeschylus, the "father of tragedy," to give birth to such a masterpiece. For my part, I didn't know whether to cry or to laugh.

Dr. Diallo believes she is going to gain credibility for the office with everyone she took the time and trouble to mention in her "evaluation" by driving a Mercedes Class-S. WHO partners were going to roll out the red carpet for her when they see her strutting around in a Mercedes-Class S. They will have no doubt that Dr. Diallo was going to take great care of the funds they are going to give WHO to achieve its main objective, that of bringing all peoples to the highest possible level of health.

Dr. Diallo also believes that she will gain credibility with the government by giving gifts to members of the Malian government. The day after we discussed the purchase of the Mercedes S-Class, Dr. Diallo called me into her office to inform me that Mali's President, Amadou Toumani Touré, wanted the WHO to give him the equivalent of five thousand US dollars (US$5,000) in fuel vouchers.

Not aware of a possible meeting between the representative and the President of Mali, I wanted to know when he asked her for that. She told me that his driver had just left her office.

Stunned by what I was hearing, I wanted to make sure that I understood what Dr. Diallo was trying to make me believe.

To do so, I asked her a question that made her burst out laughing:

- "Did the president's driver give you a paper from the presidency?"

The representative couldn't stop laughing at my gullibility. She let me know that she had never suspected that I was such a virgin.

I didn't know whether to take her words as an insult or a compliment. To ease the tense atmosphere and to avoid any deviation, I explained to her that my naivety was due to the fact that I did not attend the same school as her and that I simply wanted to understand how she could be sure that the request came from the President.

Surprised by my reaction, for which her experience and practices had not prepared her, she cut short our discussion which, according to my reactions, was certainly not going to take us where the representative wanted to go.

As I left her office, I stopped by her secretary office, who told me about how overloaded she was with work.

Since I usually ramble with her, I told her:

- "It's normal that you're too busy now that you're receiving emissaries from the President of the Republic."

Even though she was used to my jokes, Aminata looked at me as if she were seeing me for the first time and could not guess what planet I was from.

Not knowing what to answer, she asked me:

- "What republic are you talking about?"

Having guessed that I was on a slippery slope, I got straight to the point by saying:

- *"I learned that the President's driver just left the representative's office."*

After wiping away her tears that had been triggered by a fit of laughter over which she had no control, Aminata went on the offensive with the following rhetorical question:

- *"Are you jealous or what? You surprise me. Nour, I didn't know you like that. It's true that I haven't known you for long, but I think, all the same, that I know you well enough to know that you're not the jealous type."*

Impressed by Aminata's eloquence, I answered her with a tick for a tick,

- *"That's the charm of life; change, with death and taxes, are the only certainties. Thanks to this certainty, one becomes jealous at any age. There is no age limit for that."*

Afraid that the representative would come out of her office following Aminata's bursts of laughter, I asked her for permission to get down to business.

Aminata was a little surprised to learn that the representative just told me that the President's driver had just left her office. It is true that, by now, she was too familiar with Dr. Diallo's lies, but what had surprised her a little was the reason for it. Yes, she could not understand why Dr. Diallo had felt the need to tell me this lie. Not knowing the whole story, Aminata had the right to ask herself this question.

Since my intention was not to tell her the whole story, I had just heard from Dr. Diallo, I left her office telling her:

- *"Dr. Diallo told me the story because she wanted to make me jealous."*

The idea of sending fuel vouchers, in the amount of five thousand (US$5,000), to the President of Mali is Dr. Diallo trademark. I have, to this day, no reason to believe that the President of Mali made such a request. Dr. Diallo, through her experiences, came to the conclusion that everything in life is for sale. Wanting a favor from the President, she believed that fuel vouchers were an excellent commodity for barter.

This is not the first time that Dr. Diallo has used WHO funds for her own good. She paid local newspapers to publish articles that praised her skills, merits, and achievements, not those of the WHO. These newspapers published articles, or rather infomercials, of her that she had given them. Dr. Diallo was the author and the beneficiary of these so-called articles.

Dr. Diallo also paid, with WHO funds, newspapers, and radio stations, to publish and broadcast her interviews. The interview questions were prepared by Dr. Diallo herself. She therefore found herself in situations where she was answering her own questions where the focus was, of course, on her and always her.

These practices of Dr. Diallo reminded me of my Arabic literature classes, where we analyzed the poems of Arab poets who had sold their souls to the devil by constantly praising their leaders (kings, princes, etc.) in their poems.

The proliferation of this practice among these poets had given rise to a category of poetry. Part of our analysis, as students, consisted of guessing whether the poet's feelings were sincere. Of course, We had to justify our guess by taking into account the context in which the poem was written and the author's background. We learned, over time, to always say that the author's feelings were sincere if we wanted a good grade. Pink Floyd came later to question everything we have learned in those literature courses with their song "Another Brick in the Wall."

A week after my meeting with the representative, during which she had told me about the fuel vouchers to be given to the President of Mali, her secretary came to my office to tell me that the imaginary visit of the President's driver would cost the WHO five thousand American Dollars (US$5,000).

I thought that her story of five thousand (US$5,000) American dollars was more plausible as a reason for the driver's imaginary visit than the story of jealousy she wanted to pin on me in spite of my age.

I made Aminata understand my position on this matter if you can call it that by telling her:

- *"The decision to give or not to give fuel vouchers to the President of Mali was not at all up to me.*

    I do not manage any WHO programs. My role as an administration officer is limited to ensuring that WHO regulations are respected by all managers in the management of their programs.

    If a program manager submits a request to me in this regard, I will analyze it to ensure that it is consistent with the work plan, signed by WHO and the Ministry of Health, and give my opinion to the representative, in either case. She is the person who has the final word.

She is free to agree or disagree with me. She must in both cases authorize the expenditure in writing.

Therefore, I can, if necessary, ask the regional office for an opinion on the matter."

At first, I thought the representative was behaving this way with me because she thought I was unfamiliar with WHO regulations since I was new to the Organization. From my discussion with Gunther in Gaborone, I learned that flouting regulations and using civil servants as bulletproof vests were Dr. Diallo's trademarks.

Having practically failed, despite all my efforts and all my knowledge, in all my attempts to free the little Angolan girl, a modern-day slave, or to ensure the protection of the property and funds of the WHO, all that remained for me was to cover my rear.

In the November 5th, 2008 AFRO-MEMORANDUM, the subject of which is: End of your commitment, prepared meticulously and in which I am the only person concerned to be named, I was clearly informed not to set foot in my office again from that day.

The memorandum, in which the other persons concerned were designated by the acronym of their function (RPO, RD, DAF & WHO/Mali Representative), was very clear on this subject:

- *"Reference is made to your current temporary appointment with the Organization, which runs from November 10th, 2007 to November 9th, 2008. In this regard, we would like to inform you that, in accordance with Article 1040.1 of the Staff Regulations, the Organization has decided not to offer you an extension of your temporary appointment.*

Therefore, in accordance with the aforementioned Article, your commitment will end one month from receipt of this notification.

Your contract will, therefore, be revised to take this period into account.

However, you are exempt from being present at your workplace during this statutory month of notice, which will be paid to you in accordance with the provisions of Article 380.1.3 of the Staff Regulations.

In view of the above, we would be grateful if you would hand over to the WHO Representative, upon receipt of this letter, all the material and equipment of the Organization in your possession.

Attached, you will find a letter detailing the end-of-engagement formalities that you will have to complete.

Best regards."

It is very important to note that the memo announcing the non-renewal of my contract was sent by email to the representative, and not to me, who waited until the end of the day to give me a copy of the email in question.

Although it is clearly stated in the memo that, in accordance with Article 380.1.3 of the Staff Regulations, my appointment will end one month from the receipt of this notification, the representative demanded that I leave the premises immediately. I could not even take my belongings. The representative wanted to take advantage of the element of surprise to prevent me from taking with me any incriminating documents.

The next morning, I called Mr. Haarman to express my indignation, firstly, and to ask him to send an auditor to take stock of the situation before I leave Bamako for Montreal.

During the phone call that lasted more than half an hour, Mr. Haarman showed no interest in protecting the Organization's assets. Protecting WHO's reputation was also one of his least concerns. All he wanted to know was why I was insisting on sending an auditor to Bamako since he had no intention of holding me to account.

My last weeks at WHO taught me to know Mr. Haarman very well, to the point where I didn't even trust him enough to ask him what time it was. I learned to take him for what he was, but I couldn't let his last sentence go by this time.

So, I answered him decisively:

- *"I have no personal accounts to render to you. I do, however, have accounts to render to the Director of Administration and Finance of the WHO Regional Office for Africa. It so happens that this person is you. It is in that context and only in that context that I took the trouble to call you to ask you to send an auditor to take stock of the situation before my departure.*

    While the property and reputation of WHO are the least of your concerns, I place great importance on my reputation, which I have worked very hard to establish."

Seeing that I didn't call him to ask for alms, Mr. Haarman changed his tune and began to do what he does best: extract as much information as he can from the person in front of him in order to protect himself and his accomplices. He, therefore, wanted to know why I wanted him to send an auditor to Bamako.

Having no desire to discuss anything with him now that he had revealed his true nature, I answered him frankly:

- *"The auditor, if you decide to appoint one, will answer your question and many others. That is why his appointment is essential if you care about the interests, reputation, and property of WHO.*

    I am no longer employed by the WHO. Therefore, I do not have an explanation to provide to you. If you were really interested in knowing things, you could have asked me before terminating my employment. But since you know everything and you know that I know that you know everything, let's stop playing the comedy. The slightest correction requires us to have a little mutual respect.

    The Organization trusted me by offering me an administration officer contract. Now that you no longer want my services, I want to leave the Organization with a clear conscience. That is why I want you to conduct a site audit before I leave."

During our discussion, I insisted on emphasizing that the reputation of the Organization needed to be preserved in the hope of arousing Mr. Haarman's interest. He did not attach any importance to the reputation of the WHO since he did not, at any time, try to understand why I was emphasizing the reputation of the WHO in our discussion.

Convinced that Mr. Haarman would never try to understand why I was talking about the WHO's reputation, I asked him the following question:

- *"Would you be interested in knowing what is ironic about what happened yesterday?"*

Disturbed by my question, which he could not answer in the negative, he answered:

- *"If it has anything to do with work,"*

My response had indeed disturbed him:

- *"I spent the afternoon convincing Mr. Demba Doucoure, Dr. Diallo's first landlord, to withdraw the complaint he filed with the Malian Ministry of Foreign Affairs.*

    The representative had unilaterally decided to terminate the lease she had signed with him six months earlier. She had left her residence in a very poor condition, and had not paid her last month's rent and the electricity bills for May, June, July and August 2008.

    As Mr. Doucoure had had enough of the representative's contempt, he used influent people in Mali to contact the ministry of foreign affairs.

    Having made considerable progress in the discussions, we have set a meeting for today at 1:00 p.m. so we can go together to the Ministry of Foreign Affairs to withdraw his complaint and renounce contacting newspapers and radio stations during the Global Forum.

    This scandal is the last thing WHO needed two weeks before the 2nd Global Forum on Health Research.

    As a reward, the representative gave me, at the end of the day, the document informing me of the end of my contract.

    Now I think you understand why I want you to send an auditor to Bamako."

Convinced that he would never agree to carry out a site inspection, I asked him for the moon so I could obtain the earth from him. This is exactly what happened. Mr. Haarman had, in fact, agreed that I should carry out the handover to the representative.

I wanted, at least, to have a clear conscience by taking stock of the situation before leaving Bamako with a fox in the henhouse.

Needless to say, the representative had refused to let me hand over the services to her personally. She had chosen two officials to whom I had handed over the services.

Unable to free the little Angolan woman or protect the assets and funds of the WHO, I still managed to protect my rear by handing over my services. This also allowed me to keep written records of my communications and decisions (emails, reports, and meeting notes), which allowed me to write this book.

I am the first person to admit that I had lost the battle to Dr. Diallo and her accomplices, but I will never accept losing the war to her and/or her accomplices because, in my book, the fight against slavery, racism, and injustice is a perpetual fight that must never end, and it is within this framework that my current actions are taking place.

The fact that I was exempted from being present at my workplace for a month when I was paid by the WHO which needed my services during that period more than at any other period because of the 2nd Global Forum on Health Research, which was going to take place in ten days in Bamako and for which I had spent twenty-four (24) Friday afternoons preparing with the finance committee for the preparation of the Forum, is irrefutable proof that the decision not to renew my contract was taken with the sole concern of protecting the regional director.

It was, therefore, out of the question for the WHO regional management that I should be in contact with the participants in the Forum with whom I had been in permanent contact for the last three months to facilitate their arrival in Bamako. Indeed:

1. Mr. Haarman had asked me not to set foot in my office again, even though I was being paid until December 9, 2008; and

2. Someone had my house watched day and night from November 5th to December 13th, 2008, the date I left Bamako for Montreal.

On November 7th, 2008, the nightwatchman of my residence, who was finishing his shift, came to see me very early in the morning, while I was having breakfast, to tell me that he had noticed some abnormal things the last 2 nights.

I had invited him to have breakfast with me. At the table, he brought to my attention the fact that there were two people whom he had never seen before, who had spent the nights of November 5th and 6th hanging around my residence.

I asked him to call his colleague, the day watchman, who came to join us at the table for breakfast and to confirm that he indeed saw two people, unknown to him before, the morning of November 6th, who were doing rounds around my house. After discussing it among themselves, they came to the conclusion that they were not talking about the same people.

The day guard then told me:

- *I have seen the two people fifteen minutes ago. They will certainly come back. You will be able to see them with your own eyes."*

The day guard was not wrong. Less than an hour later, I saw with my own eyes these two people who did nothing to be discreet. I concluded that they were not thieves or dangerous people because if they had been, they would have taken care to try to go unnoticed and not spend two days and two nights inspecting the place.

To have a peace of mind, I called Mr. Bertin Achidi, UNDSS security officer, to inform him of what was happening around my residence. Bertin, who was not yet aware of the non-renewal of my contract, had promised me to find out what was happening and to get back to me that very morning.

Thirty minutes later, Bertin called me back to reassure me that it was the police who were ensuring my safety since the 2nd Global Forum on Health Research was going to take place in few days.

Not knowing what to say to him, I thanked him and promised to contact him if there was any problem. He thanked me and asked me to not hesitate to contact him if there was anything, even very late at night.

I could not fully accept Bertin's explanation since my contract was not renewed. I partially accepted Bertin's explanation because I thought, technically speaking, I was still employed by WHO for another month, or maybe the security arrangements were made before the date of non-renewal of my contract.

To clear my conscience, I called the other international officials at WHO to learn that there was nothing abnormal or unusual on their side. I called the administration officers of the other UN agencies. I got the same answers from them.

As if what I was experiencing was not enough for me, I now have to rewatch Alfred Hitchcock's film, *North by Northwest*, to learn how to escape this surveillance that I was seriously beginning to believe I was subject to.

While waiting to get my hands on this film to see it one more time, I came to the conclusion that I had to definitely inform the Canadian consulate in Bamako of what I was afraid of at the cost of being taken for a schizophrenic. Since I had two young children who depended on me, I preferred to be a schizophrenic but alive rather than a psychologically stable but a dead one.

I went the next morning at 10:00 to the Canadian consulate in Bamako to speak to the consul, who, after having coldly heard my story, wanted to know if I felt in danger.

My answer was clear and simple:

- *"I would be lying to you if I said that I had felt any danger or disrespect since my arrival in Mali. The situation has changed in recent days. The only disrespect I had experienced to date was the work of Dr. Soumare, a close friend of the WHO representative in Bamako.*

    Since I am a Canadian citizen and Dr. Diallo is a permanent resident of Canada, and she had asked me to find her a lawyer who would seek a Canadian citizenship for her even though she did not meet the requirements, I thought you should have this information in case something happened to me."

The consul wanted to know why I wanted to stay in Bamako since I no longer feel safe.

I calmly replied to the consul, saying:

- *"I do not want to stay in Bamako. I apologize if there was any confusion about this. I must stay in Bamako to assert*

> *my rights. I do not want the WHO to qualify my return to Montreal as an abandonment of my post."*

The consul had asked for my contact details, which I had given him. I even gave him my contact details in Canada. He then gave me his business card, encouraging me to call him if I felt that I was in any danger.

As I left his office, I was not convinced that I should leave the fate of my children in the hands of the consul. His coldness had not inspired any confidence in me. The future had confirmed my uncertainties; I have, to this day, never received the slightest call or correspondence from the consul or the consular services to find out whether I was still alive.

I had spent the weekend of November 8-9, 2008, thinking about what to do next with my life. I had finally concluded that I should go to the Consulate of the United States of America in Bamako.

The behavior of the Consulate of the United States of America in Bamako towards me in the same matter on Monday, November 10th, when I presented myself at their front door, was diametrically opposed to that of the Consulate of Canada. However, I am neither an American citizen nor a permanent resident of the United States of America. The only link I had with the United States of America was the fact that I had done my post-university studies and that I had taken my first professional steps in Philadelphia.

The trust born in the first minutes of our meeting made me empty my one-ton bag that I was miserably carrying on my back. I felt so free and light after our meeting that I didn't need to take a taxi home. I felt so happy to meet someone who had taken the time and care to listen to me that I had extended the journey that took me home. I had discovered places and a restaurant that I didn't know existed. I had probably the best pizza of my life that day.

The pizza was so good that I felt guilty eating it all by myself. When I returned to Canada more than a month later, I made sure to bring back a large pizza for each of my two children. I was sure that they would not believe me if I only told them about this pizza. So, I decided to give credibility to my story.

To my great surprise, instead of thanking me, my children had reproached me for not taking them to that restaurant when they visited me a year earlier, especially since we had the youngest son's birthday to celebrate. Otherwise, as we say in my country, do a good deed and forget it. Do a bad deed and remember it all your life.

> *I WILL GIVE*
> *my teachers, my colleagues and my students*
> *the respect and gratitude that is their due.*
>
> **- WMA Declaration of Geneva**

Having learned that I knew more than I should have known, Dr. Diallo did not want to smell my scent in the WHO office in Bamako. To achieve her goal, she did not respect any rules of conduct. She went so far as to contradict me in front of all the officials regarding the date of introduction of GSM in the WHO African region. Indeed, Dr. Diallo had clearly stated in front of all the officials that November 1st, 2008, was still the date chosen by the WHO African region for the introduction of GSM after I announced to them that the date of the launch of GSM in Africa had been postponed because of the challenges facing the WHO African region.

This statement was made by her with the sole and unique aim of contradicting me since I had announced, five minutes earlier, that given the challenges that awaited us, November 1st, 2008 is no longer the date chosen by the WHO for the introduction of GSM in the African region.

The original minutes of the October 2nd, 2008 staff meeting, sent to all staff by the secretary of the meeting on October 6th, 2008, included this statement by the Representative: *"GSM will be operational in the WHO African Region from November 1st, 2008."* This statement had magically disappeared in the amended version of the October 13th, 2008 minutes, in complete violation of the regulations governing amendments to staff meeting minutes.

Since she did not win her case with the officials, the Representative went to try her luck on a terrain that was hers, body and soul: the WHO regional management. A terrain where she would stop at nothing since no one was going to ask her for explanations and no one was going to verify the authenticity of the documents she provided as proof of her assertions.

It is in that context that she went so far as to state in her unilateral "evaluation" that I didn't understand anything of what was being said in Gaborone and that I was incapable of giving a report when the administration officer should be the basis for driving the dynamics of the important changes that should take place in the WHO program management process.

Mr. Haarman and Mr. Durao, to whom my "assessment" was addressed, had attended the Gaborone workshop. They had, of course, witnessed my participation. They had certainly seen that I had initiated the second of the seven final recommendations of the Gaborone GSM awareness workshop. At no point had they reminded the Representative of this after reading her "assessment," in which she complained about my ignorance.

Consistency seems to have deserted the Representative's dictionary for a long time. If not, how can she can assert, with all shame swallowed, in her "assessment" that *"The administration officer should be the base to drive the dynamics of the important changes that must occur in the management process of the WHO program"* when she fiercely opposed for three long weeks the participation of the administration officer in the Gaborone workshop. She had not done that last century, last decade, or last year. She had done it less than a month earlier.

Why, in light of all this, did Dr. Diallo choose a person who did not know how to use Microsoft Excel to be the foundation to drive the dynamics of the important changes that must take place in the WHO program management process?

Do not ask this question to Mr. Haarman or Mr. Durao when you are at the dinner table because their answers might take your appetite away.

This was not the first time the Representative had tried to humiliate me in front of officials. In fact, she went so far as to ask the officials who supported me to explain why they were satisfied with my work.

Dr. Ndoutabe was forced, more than once, during staff meetings, to explain his satisfaction, to the great surprise of all the other officials. When he had finished his explanation, Dr. Diallo had told him.

> - *The administration officer may be good for the private sector but not for the United Nations."*

The officials couldn't help but laugh. Thing that didn't please the Representative who ended the meeting prematurely a few minutes later.

For Dr. Diallo, everything is bought and sold in this world, even friendship. To help Dr. Soumare, a person she had introduced to me as a close friend, when our relationship was healthier, and who had taken care of her child in January 2008 before her arrival to Bamako, Dr. Diallo had decided to offer a consulting contract to her son Assane Soumare.

Wanting to help her close friend, Dr. Diallo decided to make digital archiving her first priority, although:

1. The activity was not planned, and the Office had no funds, not even for the repair of existing computer

equipment. The planned amount ($10,000) was entirely spent by the Representative on purchasing computer equipment for her own Office to replace equipment that was just over a year old.

2. The establishment of an electronic archiving system presupposes the existence of a traditional archiving system. Something that the WHO Representation Office in Mali did not have.

3. The WHO Representation office in Angola, which is much larger than that of Mali and where the Representative served as Representative before her assignment to Mali, did not feel the need to resort to digital archiving during her mandate or afterward.

4. The timing, even if there was a need, was not appropriate. Indeed:

    - The Representative and the Administration officer were new to the Office;

    - There was a transition to GSM that had to be ensured;

    - There was a Global Forum on Research for Health that had to be prepared;

    - There were also renovations of buildings to comply with the recommendations contained in the "WHO Mali security plan May 2008", prepared by Mr. Bertin Achidi, a security officer at UNDSS, in addition to the regular activities of the Office.

Despite all these facts that I brought to her attention when she raised the issue with me, Dr. Diallo made digital archiving the number one concern of the Office of the Representation of Mali, going so far as to suggest, in her August 18th, 2008 email, that the WHO risked being sued by the consultant, *"Because we prevented him from working by informing him of his selection and especially by repeatedly giving him false contract start dates."*

Dr. Diallo often appeals to her amnesia when it suits her needs. She had, in fact, intentionally forgotten to mention in her email the name of the person who notified Mr. Soumare of his selection and who gave him the false contract start dates.

One thing is certain: it wasn't me. I never informed Mr. Soumare of his selection. He knew about it before I did, and I never gave him a contract start date.

I had, however, expressed reservations because of the non-compliance with regulations and procedures in this area in what the Representative liked to call: "selection."

Indeed:

- The activity was not planned in the work plan of the WHO Representation Office in Mali;
- We had no funds to carry out an activity whose real cost we did not know;
- I did not take part in the selection process if there was ever one.
- I was the last person to know the name of the person selected or rather retained.

Once the dice were rolled, the Representative threatened me with possible legal action by the "selected" consultant, even though no commitment had been made officially, to my knowledge, by a person representing the WHO at the time the Representative's email was written.

The recruitment of Mr. Assane Soumare became problematic for Dr. Diallo when I learned that he was the son of Dr. Soumare and that I raised this issue with the Representative, telling her that I was not comfortable with the way in which he was selected and that if she really wanted to stick to her project, or rather to giving a contract to Mr. Soumare, this contract cannot, under any circumstances, be for more than one month because:

- We had no funds.
- We didn't know where we were going with this project.
- We had more important things to do, and we gave up on them due to lack of funds.
- The very conservative estimates of Mr. Yahya Coulibaly, ICT, were 9,000,000 CFA francs (approximately $20,000 U.S.) for the computer equipment plus a three (3) six (6) monthly contract for the consultant who was in his first experience in the field ($4,500 to $9,000) for a total of $24,500 to $29,000.

My proposal to offer a one-month contract, rather three or six months, having been accepted, I drafted a special services agreement which was signed on August 22nd, 2008 by Dr. Diallo and Mr. Assane Soumare. The contract in question clearly stipulated in section 1 (Terms of Reference) that the consultant was *"Under the supervision of the WHO Representative and the information technology officer."*

On Thursday, September 25th, 2008, Mr. Soumare gave me a copy of his "mission report" along with a cover letter. The document I was given was not worthy of a "digital archiving expert" (no date, no names of recipients, no contact details of the sender, etc.).

I had asked Mr. Soumare the names of the recipients of his transmission. He answered that he had given a copy to each of his two supervisors (Dr. Diallo and Mr. Yahya Coulibaly) and a copy to me because I was the administration officer. I wanted to know why he had felt the need to give me a copy of his report. His answer was simple, clear and unforgettable: "*I did it out of respect*".

I later learned that respect had to do with the actions of Mr. Soumare, who was far from being a digital archivist expert. He was nothing short of a scam expert.

On Saturday, September 27th, 2008, a weekend holiday, the Representative's secretary called me on my cell phone at 9:30 to ask me what I intended to do with Mr. Soumare's mission report, which she found too critical of the Bureau in the area of archiving.

I told her that:

> *It is up to Mr. Soumare's supervisors to evaluate the report, which I didn't read. If they ask for my opinion, I would make an effort to read it, and I would be able to give my opinion."*

On Tuesday, September 30th, 2008, Dr. Diallo called me to ask me if I received the report and the letter of transmission from Mr. Soumare because she didn't receive anything from him.

I had expressed my astonishment to her telling her that her secretary had called me on Saturday to express her opinion on the report.

I decided, after that discussion, to send her a copy of the letter of transmission and I had asked her secretary, who had expressed her bewilderment to me, to hand her a copy of the report.

On Wednesday, October 15th, 2008, Dr. Diallo sent me a letter, supposedly written by the consultant and addressed to her, in which the latter requested: "to get the remainder of my fees."

I say "supposedly written" by the consultant for the following reasons:

1. The style of this letter is completely different from the style of the transmission letter submitted by Mr. Soumare three weeks earlier;
2. The recipient's title is correct, suggesting that the letter was written by a WHO official rather than the consultant;
3. The fonts used in the two documents are completely different;
4. The signature on the letter is different from the signature on the transmittal letter of September 25th.

These facts suggest that the two letters (Letter of Transmittal and Letter of Follow-up) were not written by the same person. I do not think that one can change the writing style, the presentation of documents, and their signature within three weeks.

The Representative then ensured that the correspondence of October 15th, 2008, was exempt from reproach because this letter had only one objective, that of being added to "my assessment" as a damning piece of evidence. If not, how can one explain that **a letter dated October 15th, 2008, is cited in a report sent to Mr. Haarman on October 14th, 2008**?

In the letter she sent me, the Representative added a note in which she asked me to: "Analyze the file according to its relevance and pay the person concerned."

She also added, "ICT and I never received the file."

To which I replied:

> *Dr Diallo, the contract clearly states that Mr. Soumare is under the supervision of the WHO Representative and the Information Technology Officer. I cannot, therefore, evaluate the work of a person who does not report to me. Thank you.*"

The Representative had chosen to send, as an annex to my "evaluation," only the "original of this second letter from Mr. Soumare," which she took care to photocopy before adding her note, thus ignoring the latter and my response, in violation of all the regulations of our Organization and in complete opposition to the objectives of the management and development system of the personnel service which: "**Aims to evaluate staff in a transparent and fair manner in relation to the objectives set and to encourage them to improve themselves**."

The letter from "Mr. Soumare" and the Representative's note raises disturbing questions:

1. Assuming that the letter of October 15, 2008, came from Mr. Soumare, Is it the consultant who decides who should evaluate his work, notwithstanding the stipulations of the contract that binds him to the WHO regarding the supervision of his work?

2. The Representative should have clearly reminded the consultant that he was working under her supervision and that of the manager responsible for information and communication technologies.

3. How can the Representative assert that a person other than herself, Mr. Yahia Coulibaly, in this case, had not received the file?

a. She can make such an assertion for herself but not for another person.

b. She could assert that Mr. Yahya Coulibaly had received the report if she had been present when the report was handed over to him. But she cannot be so assertive about Mr. Coulibaly not having received the report. I believe that she should have let Mr. Yahia Coulibaly make these assertions.

c. She did not do so because Mr. Yahia Coulibaly had told me the opposite, and Mr. Soumare had told me: "I have given a copy of my report and the transmission letter to the Representative and Mr. Yahya Coulibaly, ICT."

4. Even if neither the Representative nor ICT had received the consultant's report, what would have prevented Dr. Diallo from requesting a copy of the file so that she could evaluate it or have it evaluated by Mr. Yahya Coulibaly?

5. Why did Mr. Soumare, who had worked under the supervision of Mr. Yahya Coulibaly during the month he spent in the offices of the WHO Representation, suddenly decide to submit his report to the administration officer rather than to the person who had supervised him throughout his work?

Dr. Diallo had a hot file on her hands: Mr. Soumare was not recruited according to the procedures. The report he submitted was very poorly received because of the poor quality of the work. The Representative, therefore, wanted to stick this file on me, going so far as to put forward an original argument: since Mr. Soumare had decided to give me a copy of his report, I must, therefore, evaluate it.

Dr. Diallo did not just harass me, herself; she went so far as to tell her close friend, Dr. Soumare, that I was the person who refused to pay her son. Dr. Soumare called me on my personal phone number that the Representative had given her, after my notification of the end of my engagement, to call me all the names under the sun and use words I never in my life I thought they could come out of the mouth of a medical doctor and which my decency prevents me from repeating in this book. I will, however, make one exception to say that she treated me as a "fake white man," which, according to her, is worse than a "white man".

I couldn't help to tell her that: *"If making sure the rules and regulations of WHO are respected makes me a fake white person, then I have the pleasure to enlighten you that I will be a fake white person for the rest of my life."*

The decision not to renew my temporary appointment was not motivated by my age, as suggested by Mr. Durao's letter dated October 5th, 2008, but by the need to cover for the WHO Regional Director for Africa. Dr. Diallo's evaluation report was prepared at the request of the regional management team to justify the non-renewal of my contract.

In fact, Dr Dialo evaluation report was prepared at the request of the regional Office, after deciding not to renew my appointment with WHO. But since the regulations stipulate that if my contract was not cancelled 30 working days before its expiry, it is automatically renewed for another year, my contract was therefore automatically renewed.

The regional office therefore had to overcome two obstacles:

1. There must be a very strong reason not to renew a contract that was automatically renewed;

2. There must be a very strong justification for the decision to virtually ban me from my office during the month of notice, that is, between November 5th and December 5th, 2008.

As the decision not to renew my appointment was not based on any legal foundation, RPO was very vague in its November 5th, 2008 AFRO-MEMORANDUM. RPO took care to name Article 1040.1 of the Staff Regulations to justify its decision to terminate my appointment without taking the trouble to read and understand the article in question.

Staff Rule 1040.1 clearly states that, *"Where a decision has been taken not to offer a staff member on a temporary appointment an extension, the staff member shall be notified of this fact normally not later than one month before the expiry date of the appointment."*

If the Regional Office was not going to offer me an extension of the contract, it should have told me no later than October 9th, 2008. It should also not have sent me to the GSM awareness workshop in Gaborone.

The regional Office had done none of this and had no explanation for it. RPO simply cited a sub-article of the staff regulations which includes 1,330 articles. A sub-article which did not apply to my situation at all.

RPO, who seems to care about the WHO staff regulations, has refused to date to provide me with a certificate of employment under article 1095 of the staff regulations, which clearly states:

Upon leaving the service of the Organization, every staff member shall, upon request, receive a certificate concerning the nature of his duties and the length of his service. Upon request, made in writing, the certificate shall also cover the quality of his work and his conduct in the exercise of his official functions."

Believe it or not, the WHO general office also refused to issue me such a certificate. And to think that we are in the 21st century in a specialized agency of the United Nations.

What is my crime in all this? My only and unique crime is saying no to modern-day slavery and no to child sexual abuse.

This crime earned me a report which had no evaluation other than the name that Dr. Diallo was kind enough to give it since it is much more a question of defamation, or more precisely slander, than anything else.

To achieve her aims, which consisted of ending any possibility of a career within the United Nations in general and the World Health Organization in particular, Dr. Diallo resorted to lies, half-truths and the falsification of documents which she attached as annexes to her "evaluation" and which she only made partially available to me after Mr. Haarman's intervention asking her to give me a copy of these documents as soon as possible, in accordance with the regulations and practices in this type of situation.

Dr. Diallo has brought serious and arbitrary accusations against me (violent behavior, lax behavior, disrespect, etc.) which have damaged my honor and reputation. The behavior of the WHO Representative in Mali in this matter is not worthy of a United Nations official whose General Assembly adopted on 16 December 1966 the International Covenant on Civil and Political Rights which clearly states in its Article 17:

1. No one shall be subjected to arbitrary or unlawful interference with his privacy, family, home or

correspondence, nor to unlawful attacks upon his honor and reputation.

2. Everyone has the right to the protection of the law against such interference or attacks.

> *Penso que se deve ouvir o impetrant*
> *I think the imperative should be heard*
>
> **- Dr Luis Gomes Sambo**

Dr. Sambo knew all this too well because he was involved in this story and because I made available to him all the documents supporting my statements and the documents that Dr. Diallo had falsified in full view of everyone because she knew that she was protected.

Dr. Diallo had acquired her protection in 1999 in Harare, Zimbabwe where she had begun her rise in WHO. Protection and rise that she had acquired for services rendered not to the World Health Organization but to a person who occupied, at the time, the position of WHO Program Management Director. This person became, a few years later, the WHO Regional Director for Africa.

The proof of what I am saying is contained in all the decisions taken by the regional office and the decisions that the regional office did not want to take because taking them meant exposing the regional director by exposing what guaranteed the protection of the Representative despite all her actions. These actions included the practice of modern-day slavery.

The content of Dr. Sambo's December 13th, 2008 email is an eloquent confirmation. Dr. Sambo, in fact, masterfully managed to summarize the situation in one sentence in his response to an email that I had sent the same day to Mr. Durao and where Dr. Sambo wasn't copied.

Dr. Sambo felt the need to respond to an email that was not intended for him, while he was on a mission outside the continent, because he had started to feel the heat. I wonder to this day who felt the need to forward the email to him, Dr. Diallo or Mr. Durao? Having felt the heat, Dr. Sambo could not afford to let the fire take hold in the house because he was inside that house. He had called on his compatriot, Mr. Durao, to contain the fire.

My email, written in French, to Mr. Durao was very clear. The translation of this email reads as follows:

From: N B [mailto:yassirem@yahoo.com]
To: Durao, Mr. Alvaro - bzv
Cc: MALI - WR (Diallo, Dr, Fatoumata Binta - ml)

Sent: Saturday. December 13, 2008 21:13

Good morning, Mr. Durao,

I am preparing to leave Bamako this evening to return home to Montreal, and I still didn't receive any news from you regarding my November 5th, 2008 email in which I asked you to please contact me to discuss my concerns following your memo of the same day in which you clearly stated that you remain at my disposal for any information I may need.

I find it unfortunate and regrettable that you did not take the time to contact me to clarify the things contained in your memos informing me of your decision not to renew my employment contract with WHO. A decision that was motivated by the "unilateral evaluation" submitted to you by the WHO representative in Mali under conditions that you know as well as I do. An evaluation is an evaluation in name only since it is much more defamation than anything else.

To achieve her goal, the WHO representative in Mali resorted to lies, half-truths and the falsification of documents that she attached as annexes to her "evaluation" and that she only made partially available to me after the intervention of Mr. Sander E. Haarman asking her to give me a copy of these documents as soon as possible in accordance with the regulations and practices in this type of situation.

Knowing the practices of the Representative, having worked with her for ten months, I am still not convinced that she gave me all the documents that she made available to you as part of this exercise.

You agree with me that in light of all this, I may have concerns that I want to discuss with you.

Things being what they are today and taking into account the seriousness of the false accusations made against me, I wish to inform you that I intend to respond in detail to the "assessment" of the Representative as soon as I have consulted with my legal advisor. I will do everything humanly possible to set the record straight and maintain my reputation and my dignity that I have spent so many years building. I also intend to send you a copy of the report of my time at the WHO representation office in Mali so that you can appreciate the conditions in which I had to carry out the tasks of administration officer.

Please accept, Mr. Durao, the expression of my distinguished greetings.

Dr. Sambo used just one sentence, written in Portuguese, to make the HR manager aware of the situation. A sentence that summed up all his thoughts and his dismay.

From: Sambos, Luis (sambol@who.int)
To: yassirem@yahoo.com; Da Silva Durao, MR Alvaro J. – Afro
CC: Haarman, Mr. Sander Edward - Afro

DATE: Saturday December 23, 2008, 15 H 50 Min 23 S

OBJECT: RE: End of contract

RPO

Penso que se deve ouvir o impetrante.

Saudacoes.

L. Sambo RD / AFRO

Sent from a BB Terminal"

His email can be translated as follows, *"RPO, I think the imperative should be heard. Greetings."*

Yes, Dr. Sambo knew that he was in trouble in this matter and the fact that he was on a mission outside the continent had further complicated things for him. Unable to put out the fire remotely that day, he had tried to contain it. He wanted to buy time and that is why he had copied me in the email he had sent to Mr. Durao.

It is very important to note that Dr. Diallo, a person very concerned by the case, was not copied in Dr. Sambo's email. Transparency seems to be lacking at the WHO Regional Director and Regional Office for Africa.

Mr. Durao knew very well what the regional director expected from him and had played the game very well. It was a game that consisted of dragging things out in order to later invoke the argument of time limits because if I had to contest the decision of the regional office, I would have to do so within 60 days of receiving the decision.

Mr. Durao played his game very well. He did not disappoint Dr. Sambo, who knew he could count on him, having played in the same team for a long time.

Mr. Durao immediately took the fire extinguisher and took action by sending me the following timer, which I am translating below:

FROM: duraoalv@afro.who.int
TO: yassirem@yahoo.com
   CC: haarmans@afro.who.int, sambol@afro.who.int, diallof@ml.afro.who.int

DATE: December 15, 2008, 02H 26M

OBJECT: RE: END OF CONTRACT

Dear Mr. Benakezouh,

I am sorry that I was not able to contact you as agreed, but I have been away from Brazzaville for the past few weeks (I returned this Sunday, December 14, from Kuala Lumpur).

Please note that you can call me on my mobile number (002427700200), or you can give me a number where I can reach you this week.

I'm leaving on Friday for vacation and won't be back until January 5, 2009.

Best regards.

Alvaro Durao, RPO"

Mr. Durao's response is worthy of a reaction of six-year-old caught red-handed. Mr. Durao had access to his email from all four corners of the world. Why wait to return to Brazzaville to respond to such an urgent email?

Subsequent events confirmed that his 'absence' from Brazzaville, if true, had nothing to do with Mr. Durao's delay in responding to my urgent email. The latter's behavior is similar to that of a football player who is leading the score and wasting time while waiting for the referee to blow the final whistle.

On the same day, I sent the following email to Mr. Durao:

FROM: yassirem@yahoo.com
TO: duraoalv@afro.who.int
CC: haarmans@afro.who.int

DATE: MONDAY, JANUARY 15, 2008, 18 H 59

OBJECT: RE: END OF CONTRACT

Good morning, Mr. Durao,

I am in Montreal (GMT - 5) since yesterday.

My phone numbers are:

Landline: 1 514 327 2152

Mobile: 1 514 825 4723

Greetings

Nour E. Benakezouh, MBA
yassirem@yahoo.com

Needless to say, that Mr. Durao never felt the need to return my calls or call me as he promised to do. His actions speak volumes.

Modern Day Slavery

Having had confirmation that Mr. Durao was wasting time, I sent him an email on January 18th, 2009, in which I could not have been clearer:

>
> FROM: yassirem@yahoo.com
> TO: duraoalv@afro.who.int
> CC: haarmans@afro.who.int
>
> DATE: SUNDAY, JANUARY 18, 2009, 18 H 01
>
> OBJECT: RE: END OF CONTRACT
>
> Dear Mr. Durao,
>
> *My legal advisors and I are in the process of finalizing my response to the unilateral "assessment" of the WHO Representative in Mali. We are faced with the fact that documents referred to by Dr. Diallo in her "assessment" have not been provided to me. In order to avoid any confusion, I would be grateful if you could send me a copy of all the documents concerning me that were provided to you by the Representative in order to provide you with the most complete response.*
>
> *Distinguished greetings*
>
> *Nour E. Benakezouh, MBA*
> *yassirem@yahoo.com* "

Seeing that Mr. Durao didn't give a damn about my correspondence, I decided to send him a final email. I took the time and care to send a copy of the email to the regional director.

FROM: yassirem@yahoo.com
TO: duraoalv@afro.who.int
CC: haarmans@afro.who.int

DATE: MONDAY, JANUARY 26, 2009, 15 H 59

OBJECT: RE: END OF CONTRACT

Dear Mr. Durao,

Despite your 15-12-2008 email in which you stated your availability to respond to my concerns regarding the non-renewal of my contract, my 15 12-2008 and 18 01 -2009 emails have remained, to this day, unanswered by you.

As I mentioned to you in my 13-12-2008 email, I intend to do everything humanly possible to set the record straight and maintain my reputation and dignity that I have spent so many years building.

The false accusations of the WHO Representative in Mali and the falsification of the documents she gave you are quite serious matters in my book, and I am still convinced that they are also serious in the books of the World Health Organization. This is why I asked you in my 18-01-2009 email to kindly send me a copy of all the documents concerning me that were given to you by the Representative who, despite the intervention of Mr. Haarman asking her to give me a copy of these documents as soon as possible in accordance with the regulations and practices in this type of situation, only made part of the documents in question available to me.

The Representative has taken care not to number the documents she has given you for the sole purpose of making any verification difficult. Having worked with Dr Diallo for almost ten months, I have learned all her maneuvers and shenanigans. In a word, I am vaccinated against them.

For the moment I am contented to communicate with you personally because I am convinced that it is in my interest as well as that of the WHO to seek the truth in this episode.

If for some reason this conviction evaporates, I will have no other choice than to hand over the entire file to my lawyers.

Distinguished greetings

Nour E. Benakezouh, MBA
yassirem@yahoo.com

The fact of having copied Dr. Sambo in my January 26th, 2009 email seems to have borne fruit since on January 27th, 2009, the gentleman finally responded to my last correspondence by sending me the following email:

FROM: duraoalv@afro.who.int
TO: yassirem@yahoo.com
CC: haarmans@afro.who.int, sambol@afro.who.int, director-general@who.int

SENT: TUESDAY JANUARY 27, 2009, 10 h 19

OBJECT: RE: END OF CONTRACT

Dear Mr. Benakezouh,

We are currently compiling the requested documents in order to send them to you.

Best regards.

Alvaro Durao RPO

One wonders how long this compilation would take. My request was made on October 14th, 2008. 135 days later, Mr. Durao and his team are still compiling the documents.

Mr. Durao was very stingy with explanations in his email after more than six weeks of radio silence. This silence was dictated by the need to make me exceed the 60-day deadline, during which I had to submit my opposition to the regional office's decision not to renew my contract.

Last, but not least, One should notice that Dr. Diallo is not copied in the emails of Mr. Durao anymore.

FROM: yassirem@yahoo.com
TO: duraoalv@afro.who.int
Cc: haarmans@affo.who.int, sambol@afio.who.int, director-general@who.int

SENT: SUNDAY SEPTEMBER 13, 2009, 15 h 12 min 45 s

OBJECT: RE: END OF CONTRACT

Good morning, Mr. Durao,

I have been waiting for your phone call since December 15th, 2008, the date on which I gave you my telephone numbers as you requested in your email of the same day.

As I mentioned to you in my December 13th, 2008 email, the day before leaving Bamako, the Representative made serious and defamatory accusations against me and I intend to do everything humanly possible to set the record straight and maintain my reputation and dignity that I have spent so many years building.

Since the steps I am taking to clear my name do not seem to be as important to you as they are to me, I would be grateful if you could send me:

- *A certificate concerning the nature of my duties, the duration of my services, the quality of my work, and my conduct in the exercise of my official duties;*
- *A copy of the procedure(s) for appealing the decision of the WHO Regional Director.*

Please accept, Mr. Durao, my distinguished greetings.

*Nour E. Benakezouh, MBA
yassirem@yahoo.com*

Mr. Durao's lack of seriousness is disgusting. One only has to read his emails sent the same day, in response to my email sent ten days earlier and three reminders sent between September 13th and September 23rd, 2009, to realize this.

On Wednesday, September 23rd, 2009 at 08:30 am, eleven months after leaving Bamako, Mr. Durao decided to provide me with a work certificate. He told me in his email that, "The certificate will reach you shortly".

*FROM: duraoalv@afro.who.int
TO: yassirem@yahoo.com
CC: haarmans@afro.who.int, sambol@afro.who.int, director-general@who.int*

SENT: WEDNESDAY, SEPTEMBER 23, 2009, 15 H 31

OBJECT: RE: END OF CONTRACT

> Dear Mr. Benakezouh,
>
> I was informed by my colleagues that the requested certificate was sent to you last week.
>
> Best regards,
>
> Alvaro Durao RPO"

My certificate was so heavy that it took more than one nameless colleague to send it to me.

Since ridicule does not kill, I received the next day an email from Mr. Wadda with, as an attachment, a certificate signed by Mr. Durao. A question arises of itself: why did Mr. Durao use the services of Mr. Wadda to send me a document that he just signed and which, according to him, had already been sent to me? Quite simply because he went to the same school as Dr. Diallo. He needed someone to blame for the deliberate delays they were putting in responding to my emails.

Tired of Mr. Durao's behavior, I sent him an email to inform him that the certificate, which was sent to me by Mr. Wadda and signed by himself, was not at all in accordance with Article 1095 of the Staff Regulations and Staff Status, in force since July 2007, which clearly states:

"1095. CERTIFICATION OF SERVICE

> *A staff member who so requests shall, on leaving the service of the Organization, be given a certificate relating to the nature of his duties and the length of his service. On written request of the staff member concerned, the certificate shall also refer to the quality of his performance and official conduct.*"

Eleven months after leaving WHO, I was still without a work certificate that complied with the regulations. This situation had a devastating effect on my job search because I was always asked after the interview to provide the name of my supervisor or a copy of my work certificate at WHO. I was unable to do so or explain to them why I could not do so because I could not ask people to understand what I, myself, could not understand. In any case, no one would have believed me if I had tried to explain to them the situation, I found myself in while trying to free a thirteen-year-old Angolan girl.

> *FROM: yassirem@yahoo.com*
> *TO: duraoalv@afro.who.int*
> *Cc: haarmans@affo.who.int, sambol@afio.who.int, director-general@who.int*
>
> SENT: THURSDAY SEPTEMBER 24, 2009, 16 h 07 min 45 s
>
> OBJECT: RE: END OF CONTRACT
>
> Dear Mr. Durao,
>
> *Mr. Wadda has indeed sent me a certificate signed by you, but it does not comply with my request in the sense that this certificate makes no mention of the quality of my work and my conduct in the exercise of my official functions. I therefore ask you to send me a certificate in accordance with Article 1095 of the Staff Regulations and Staff Rules, in force since July 2007.*
>
> Best regard
>
> *Nour E. Benakezouh, MBA*
> *yassirem@yahoo.com"*

Mr. Durao did not send me an acknowledgement of receipt of my September 24th email and turned a deaf ear to my five other reminders (October 6th, 13th, 20th, November 3rd & 10th, 2009).

This contempt on the part of Dr. Sambo, Mr. Durao & Mr. Haarman has meant that sixteen years later, I am still without a

Modern Day Slavery

certificate in accordance with Article 1095 of the Staff Regulations and Staff Regulations of the World Health Organization and that Dr. Diallo has never been worried despite all her actions. It is hard to believe that all this is happening in a specialized agency of the United Nations.

To be free is not merely to cast off one's chains but to live in a way that respects and enhances the freedom of others.

— Nelson Mandela

Seeing thatMr. Durao did not care about my objective of setting the record straight in this matter and convinced that Dr. Diallo was not going to do it, I sent a 53-page letter with 97 annexes to Dr, on October 11, 2009, for the sake of conscience.

In this letter, I took the care and time to respond in the slightest details, with evidence, documents, names and contact details of witnesses to support the lies, half-truths, falsification of documents, and defamation of Dr. Diallo.

October 19th, 2009

Dr Luis G. Sambo
WHO Regional Director for Africa
Cite du Djoue, P.O.Box 06
Brazzaville, Congo

Object: *Request for review of the decision to terminate my temporary appointment*

Mr. The Director,

On November 5th, 2008, Mr. Alvaro Durao, Regional Personnel Officer, provided me, through the WHO Representative in Mali, Dr Fatoumata Binta Diallo, a memorandum terminating my appointment with the World Health Organization in accordance with Staff Regulation

1040.1 and another memorandum on the subject of appointment formalities.

These two memos were prepared with such haste that the Regional Personnel Officer, Mr. Alvaro Durao, sent them to me under the cover of the Representative of Burkina Faso and wished me, on your behalf, a good and healthy retirement.

The decision not to renew my temporary appointment was not motivated by my age but rather by the "Evaluation" Report of the Representative of the Mali Bamako Country Office, prepared by the WHO Representative in Mali and dated October 14th, 2008.

This report, as I mentioned in my previous correspondence to Mr. Alvaro Durao, with copies to you and to Mr. Haarman, had nothing of an evaluation other than the name that Dr Diallo was kind enough to give it since it is much more of a defamation than anything else.

Indeed, in order to achieve her aims, which consisted of ending any career in the United Nations system in general and the World Health Organization in particular, the Representative resorted to lies, half-truths, and the falsification of documents which she attached as annexes to her "evaluation" and which she only made partially available to me after Mr. Haarman's intervention asking her to give me a copy of these documents as soon as possible, in accordance with the regulations and practices in this type of situation.

The Representative brought serious and arbitrary accusations against me (violent behavior, lax behavior, disrespect, etc.) with the only aim to damage my honor and reputation.

The behavior of the WHO Representative in Mali in this matter is not worthy of a United Nations official whose General Assembly adopted on December 16th, 1966, the International Covenant on Civil and Political Rights, which stipulates in its Article 17:

1. *No one shall be subjected to arbitrary or unlawful interference with his privacy, family, home, or correspondence, nor to unlawful attacks on his honor and reputation.*

2. *Everyone has the right to the protection of the law against such interference or attacks.*

Therefore, I kindly ask you to:

1. *Review your decision to terminate my temporary engagement;*

2. *Declare null and void the "Evaluation Report of the Administration officer of the Mali-Bamako Country Office"; and*

3. *Remove this report from my administrative file.*

My present request is justified by the fact that the Representative ignored all the rules and regulations of the Organization by:

1. *Not establishing an activity plan based on individual goals for myself;*

2. *Refusing to meet me to assess me, claiming that I refused to be assessed despite my emails stating my availability for the assessment;*

3. *Submitting an arbitrary "Evaluation Report;" refusing, initially, to provide me with the annexes attached to his "evaluation report;"*

4. *Only giving me part of these annexes even after Mr. Haarman's intervention asking her to "give me a copy as soon as possible in accordance with the regulations and practices in this type of situation," thus denying me the right to know the accusations brought against me.*

The information that Dr. Diallo has submitted to you is nothing but lies and, at best, half-truths. Some of the documents included in the Annexes are falsified and others are simply created from scratch by Dr. Diallo to confirm her claims.

I am attaching to this letter my response to the "Evaluation" Report of the Administration officer of the Mali-Bamako Country Office. The assertions contained in my report are supported by 97 documents that I am attaching as annexes.

The time taken to provide me with the annexes to the assessment report and the seriousness of the accusations made against me by the Representative, especially those concerning the violent behavior of which she accused me of, forced me to take the time necessary to seek help from those close to me to decide on the appropriate response to these accusations and to compile file as complete as possible.

Convinced of the importance that you will give to my present request; I remain available for any additional information that could help you make a fair and an informed decision.

Please accept, Mr. Director, my distinguished greetings.

Nour E. Benakezouh, MBA
yassirem@yahoo.com

The Regional Director did not see fit to respond to my request to review the regional office's decision. He did even better than that; he did not even consider it necessary to acknowledge receipt of my request. Impressive when you consider that this is the same person who took the trouble on December 13th, 2008, while he was out of the continent, to respond to an email that was not addressed to him and for which he was not even copied.

The person who thought on December 13th, 2008 that I deserve to be heard no longer thinks so on October 11th, 2009. Why did Dr. Sambo change his mind?

Because he now believes that his accomplice had succeeded in his game of delaying things. Now he can assert the 60-day limitation period that I had to assert my rights.

Once I had the rules and procedures for Appeal of the Regional Office for Africa in hand, I wrote my memorandum of the decision not to extend my appointment which I had submitted to the Regional Appeals Committee on January 25th, 2010.

January 25, 2010

Mr. Pule
President of the Regional Appeals Committee
World Health Organization
Regional Office for Africa

Object: *Appeal of the decision not to renew my temporary contract*

Mr. Pule,

I respectfully submit to the Regional Appeals Committee, which you chair, a copy of my appeal briefs against the decision, not to extend my temporary contract.

I declare and argue in this brief that the Administration's decision not to offer me an extension of my temporary contract results from:

- *The bias is shown to my detriment by my immediate superior;*
- *The Administration's incomplete examination of the facts submitted by my immediate superior,* and
- *The failure to comply, among other things, with articles 530.1 and 530.2 of the Staff Regulations and Regulations.*

I am convinced that I am not the only one who suffers harm when the Administration does not follow its own rules, as it is supposed to. The entire administrative process is actually undermined when my due process rights are seriously affected.

Scrupulously and irreproachably respecting the procedure established by the Administration is the prerequisite and essential condition for the proper functioning of any administrative justice system.

Pending a favorable response to my present request, I ask the members of the Regional Appeal Committee to accept my distinguished greetings. I remain available for any information or document you may need for the evaluation of my request.

Nour E. Benakezouh, MBA

yassirem@yalroo.com

The response from the regional office was not long in coming since it was very simple. Mr. Durao now has time to respond since his response, in addition to being dishonest, is pathetic.

Mr. Durao, who had spent a whole year delaying things by not responding to my emails and phone calls, by keeping none of his promises, and by flouting all WHO rules and regulations on personnel management, allows himself, with all shame, to invoke the provisions of Article 1230.8.3 of the Staff Rules, to argue that my appeal is inadmissible.

Reading his argument, I could not help but feel sorry for Africans whose health destiny is partially in the hands of people like Mr. Durao.

I can't say more than that because I can't find the words that qualify Mr. Durao's arguments. I will let find those words by letting you read his response to my appeal. Response that I took the liberty to translate from French to English.

AFRO-MEMORANDUM

From: Alvaro
To: Thebe A. Pule
Date: 02/02/2010 RPO Chairperson

Ref: Memorandum 0f 28/01/10

Object: Appeal filed by Mr. Nour-Eddine Benakezouh

Further to your memorandum referenced above, relating to the appeal lodged with the AFRO Regional Appeals Committee by Mr. Nour-Eddine Benakezouh, I hereby inform you of the position of the Administration of the AFRO Regional Office with regard to the arguments raised by the interested party in support of his appeal.

I. THE FACTS

Mr. Nour-Eddine Benakezouh was recruited on November 10, 2007, as an international temporary staff member to serve as an Administration officer in the WHO Representation Office in Mali. Mr. Benakezouh temporary appointment was scheduled for a period of one year, from November 10, 2007, to November 9, 2008. On November 5, 2008, a memorandum was sent to the staff member notifying him that his temporary contract would not be extended in accordance with Staff Rule 1040.

In order to comply with the provisions which, require that the non-extension of the contract of a member of staff hired on a temporary basis be notified to him at least one month before the end of the contract, the contract was extended until December 6 2008.

II. CONCLUSION AND RECOMMENDATIONS

A temporary appointment is, by definition, limited in time and automatically expires at the end of the agreed period of service. The temporary appointment contract, which was accepted and signed by Mr. Benakezouh, explicitly states that "in the absence of any offer and acceptance of an extension, temporary appointments shall automatically terminate upon completion of the agreed period of service" (copy attached).

In support of his appeal against the decision not to extend his temporary contract, Mr. Nour-Eddine Benakezouh invokes reasons exclusively related to the procedure for evaluating his performance during his period of activity at the WHO Representation Office in Mali. However, this reason is not mentioned in the memorandum of November 5th, 2008. At no time did the WHO Administration give reasons for the non-extension of Mr. Benakezouh temporary contract based on performance.

Accordingly, we consider that the reasons given by Mr. Benakezouh in support of his appeal against the decision not to extend his temporary contract are null and void.

Furthermore, according to the provisions of Article 1230.8.3 of the Staff Regulations, an appeal by a staff member concerning a final decision of the Administration must be made no later than 60 calendar days following the date of actual receipt of notification of the decision. However, Mr. Benakezouh present appeal is dated January 25 2010 and concerns a decision not to extend a temporary contract which was notified to him on November 5 2008.

Mr. Benakezouh appeal is therefore inadmissible.

Warmest greetings

On February 10th, 2010, I gathered my courage with both hands to respond to Mr. Durao's argument. It took, indeed, great courage to accept Mr. Durao's challenge. Debating is probably one of my favorite activities in life when the game is worth the candle, which is far from being the case here. I did it, however, reluctantly by sending the following letter to the President of the Regional Appeals Committee:

February 10, 2010

Mr. Thebe A. Pule
President of the Regional Appeals Committee
World Health Organization
Regional Office for Africa

Object: *Response to the position of the Administration of the WHO Regional Office for Africa (Case 006/2010)*

Mr. Pule,

I acknowledge receipt of your correspondence of February 4th, 2010, in which you sent me a copy of the response from the Administration of the WHO Regional Office for Africa to your request following the appeal that I lodged with the Regional Appeals Committee.

I am sending you my response to the conclusions and recommendations of the Administration.

I ask you, as well as all the members of the RAC, to accept my distinguished greetings and remain available for any information or any additional document which you would need for the evaluation of my request.

Nour-Eddine Benakezouh, MBA
yassirem@yahoo.com

RESPONSE TO THE ADMINISTRATION'S POSITION

Discretionary power of the Administration

It is true that, according to case law, a civil servant holding a temporary appointment is not, generally speaking, entitled to count on an extension. The Administration has the discretionary power not to extend a temporary appointment.

Indeed, the United Nations Administrative Tribunal has repeatedly held that the Administration has discretionary power in the matter of renewal or non-renewal of an appointment and that an appointment, if not renewed, terminates with the passage of time as provided for in the appointment itself. **(Judgments No. 440, Shankar (1989) and No. 1003, Shasha's (2001).**

However, the established jurisprudence of the United Nations Administrative Tribunal is that the exercise of this discretionary power must not be tainted by caprice, bias, falsehood, or serious breach of due process. This discretionary power must be exercised without the intervention of any improper motivation so as to avoid an abuse of power **(Judgments No. 50, Brown, No. 142, Bhattacharyya; No. 109, Shields, No. 319, Jekhine, and No. 345, Najar).**

The United Nations Administrative Tribunal stated in its **Judgment No. 885** *that the exercise by the Administration of its discretionary power not to renew a contract must not be vitiated* *by any form of abuse of authority and that in the presence of special circumstances, in particular in cases of misuse by the Administration of its discretionary power in refusing to renew a contract, the United Nations Administrative Tribunal considered that an exception could be made to the rule of discretionary power.*

The United Nations Administrative Tribunal has also held that a staff member could, in the circumstances of the case, reasonably expect to be considered for renewal even when the non-renewal was without justification **(Judgment 1254)**.

The question that arises, in light of the established case laws of the United Nations Administrative Tribunal on contract renewal, is therefore whether the Administration's decision not to renew my appointment was vitiated by any form of abuse of power (arbitrariness, irregularity of procedure, irregularity of motivation, other extrinsic motivations).

I maintain that the Administration's decision not to renew my temporary appointment was vitiated by the abuse of power of my superior, who submitted a one-sided "evaluation report" riddled with lies, half-truths, and false documents, in complete violation of the Staff Regulations and Rules.

The fact that no mention of my evaluation, my performance and my behavior is made in the memorandum of November 5th, 2008 is far from being proof that the Administration's decision was not motivated by the "evaluation report" of my hierarchical superior.

Aware that my supervisor had violated WHO's Rules and Procedures on evaluation, the Administration did not want to refer to my supervisor's "Evaluation Report" in its decision not to renew my appointment. To avoid any questioning of its decision not to renew my appointment, the Administration therefore opted to use its discretionary power. By doing so, the Administration wanted to deprive me of my right to appeal the decision not to extend my appointment.

After denying me the right to respond to the false allegations made against me by my superior by making a decision based on a unilateral "evaluation report," the Administration now wants to deprive me of my right of appeal by arguing the notion of the discretionary power of the Administration.

In its **Judgment No. 733**, the United Nations Administrative Tribunal stated that "**It is a fundamental principle of law that everyone has the right to be heard in his or her case and to be given an opportunity to respond to the allegations made against him or her. By failing to provide this right, the Respondent has failed in its obligation to respect due process towards the applicant.**"

An analysis of the facts leading up to and following the Administration's decision not to renew my appointment will show that this decision is tainted by bias, falsehoods, and a breach of due process.

The Administration cannot, therefore, rely on the rule of discretionary power to legitimize a decision vitiated by forms of abuse of power.

On August 26th, 2008, Ms. Marie Louise Omog sent an email to the Country Office Representatives and Administration officers containing attached the list of participants in the sensitization and training workshop for Country Office

Representatives and Administration officers in Gaborone, Botswana (18-22 September 2008). **My name was on this list**.

The great importance of the GSM workshop, the implementation of which will considerably change the way WHO Country Offices operate, is explained in the document prepared by Mr. Andres Nzang.

The launch of GSM in the African region was scheduled for November 1, 2008 (4 days before the end of my temporary appointment and 25 days after the date on which the Administration was to notify me of the non-renewal of my appointment in the event that my appointment was not to be renewed).

On August 29th, 2008, following the intervention of my superior with Afro to remove my name from the list of participants, Mrs. Marie Louise Omog sent an email to the Country Office Representatives and Administration officers containing as an attachment the final list of participants in the sensitization and training workshop for Country Office Representatives and Administration officers in Gaborone, Botswana (18-22 September 2008). **My name was not on this list.**

The same day, I sent an email to Dr. Oladapo Walker informing him that my name was not on the August 29th list while it was on the August 26th list.

Having received no response from Dr Oladapo Walker, I sent another email on August 30th, 2008 to Mrs. Marie Louise Omog asking her why I was the only administration officer in Africa whose name did not appear on the 29th August list of *participants in the Gaborone GSM Sensitization and Training Workshop.*

On September 1st, 2008, Mr. Andres Nzang sent an email to the Country Office Representatives and Administration officers containing attached the final list of participants in the awareness raising and training workshop for Country Office Representatives and Administration officers in Gaborone, Botswana (18-22 September 2008). **My name was put back on the list.**

In this email, Mr. Andres Nzang clearly wrote, "Following the guidance of the Regional Director, please find attached the final list of participants for the workshop mentioned in the subject line."

Not content with my name being put back on the final list of participants for the sensitization and training workshop for Representatives and Administration officers of the country offices in Gaborone, Botswana (18-22 September 2008), my superior spent the next fifteen days making representations to Afro to prevent me from participating in this workshop because she had already unilaterally decided to get rid of me at the end of my engagement.

Her September 2nd, 2008 email (1 day after receiving the memo from Mr. Andres Nzang) is proof of my superior's determination to keep me away from this workshop and therefore to terminate my engagement.

October 5th, 2008 (one month before the end of my contract) is the date on which the Administration was to notify me of the non-renewal of my contract in the event that my contract was not renewed (article 1040.1 of the Staff Regulations and Rules).

On October 10th, 2008, my superior, not seeing the decision not to renew my appointment, sent an email to Mr. Haarman with copies to Mr. Durao and Mr. Wadda asking them to: "note that the start date of Mr. Nour's contract is November 9th, 2007 instead of the 14th". The Representative did not consider it useful to send me a copy of this email.

On October 11th, 2008, Mr. Haarman sent an email to my supervisor and Mr. Durao, with a copy to Mr. Wadda, stating, "This is noted, and we will therefore study your evaluation report upon receipt. Please do not forget to copy the person concerned."

It is clear that, as of October 11th, 2008, the decision not to renew my contract was not yet taken, although October 5th, 2008, was the date on which the Administration was to notify me of the non-renewal of my contract in the case that my appointment was not to be renewed. Mr. Haarman even informed my supervisor that he would study his evaluation report upon receipt."

On October 14th, 2008, my superior sent him a unilateral "Evaluation Report" to AFRO, with a copy to me.

On October 15th, 2008, I sent an email to my supervisor, Mr. Haarman and Mr. Durao with a copy to Mr. Wadda acknowledging receipt of the "Evaluation Report" and promising a response to my supervisor's allegations by Monday, October 20th "if I would receive the annexes by then."

On October 20th, 2008, my superior sent the annexes of her unilateral "Evaluation Report" to AFRO. My superior refused to give me a copy of these annexes despite my request in the email of October 15th.

On October 22md, 2008, I sent an email to Mr. Haarman and Mr. Durao, with copies to my supervisor and Mr. Wadda, apologizing for not sending my response to my supervisor's allegations because I had still not received a copy of the annexes.

Seeing nothing forthcoming, I called Mr. Haarman on Saturday, October 25th, 2008, and left a message in his voicemail informing him that I had still not received the annexes and could, therefore, not adequately respond to my superior's accusations.

On October 27th, 2008, Mr. Haarman sent an email to my superior asking her to "give me a copy of the annexes as soon as possible in accordance with the regulations and practices in this type of situation."

On November 3rd, 2008, my superior gave me a copy of the annexes in question. My first surprise was to see that the annexes were not numbered.

On November 5th, 2008, as I was preparing to respond to my superior's allegations, the Administration provided me, through my superior, with a memorandum informing me of their decision not to renew my appointment.

The same day, as soon as I received the memorandum, I called Mr. Durao several times by telephone to obtain an explanation regarding the termination without success. Not being able to reach him phone, I sent him an email by the end of the day.

Between November 17th and 19th, 2008, the Global Ministerial Forum on Research for Health took place, of which I was a member of the organizing committee.

On December 13th, 2008, I sent an email to Mr. Durao, with copies to Mr. Haarman and Dr. Fatoumata Binta Diallo, in which I clearly denounced the abuse of power by my superior (lies, half-truths, and falsification of documents). I informed Mr. Durao that I intend to respond in detail to the "assessment" of the Representative as soon as I have consulted with my legal advisor. I intend to do everything humanly possible to set the record straight and maintain the reputation and dignity that I have spent so many years building.

The same day, Dr. Sambo sent an email to Mr. Durao and me with a copy to Mr. Haarman, in which he said verbatim, "RPO Penso que se deve ouvir o impetrante."

Translation: "I think we should hear the petitioner."

On December 15th, 2008, Mr. Durao sent me an email saying he was sorry he had not been able to contact me and asking me to provide him with a telephone number where he could call me.

The same day, I sent an email to Mr. Durao, and I gave him my telephone numbers in Montreal.

On January 19th, 2009, I sent an email to Mr. Durao, with a copy to Mr. Haarman, asking him to send me a copy of the annexes submitted by my superior with her "Evaluation Report" since, like me, my legal counsel suspected that there were annexes missing. The fact that my superior had not numbered the annexes complicated matters considerably.

On January 29th, 2009, Mr. Éric Tagnon, on Mr. Durao's instructions, sent me an email with the annexes I had requested. A check of these annexes proved to me that some annexes were indeed missing. I understood at that time why the annexes were not numbered and why my superior had refused to give them to me at first and then to give me only part of them.

Having received no call from Mr. Durao, contrary to what he had promised me in his email of December 15th, 2008, and noting that my efforts did not seem as important to the administration as they were to me, I sent an email to Mr. Durao on September 13th, 2009, reminding him that I was still waiting for his phone call and my determination to follow through on this matter. I also asked Mr. Durao to send me a certificate regarding the nature of my duties, the length of my service, the quality of my work, and my conduct in the exercise of my official duties, as well as a copy of the procedure(s) for appealing the decision of the Regional Director.

On September 23rd, 2009, Mr. Wadda sent me an email with an attached certificate. Please note that for reasons unknown to me, Mr. Wadda did not finish his sentence in which he gave the conditions for the extension of my appointment.

On the same day, the regional office sent me a copy of the part of the Staff Regulations and Rules concerning appeal committees and not the rules and procedures of the Regional Appeal Committee.

On September 24th, 2009, I sent an email to Mr. Durao informing him that the certificate sent to me was not in accordance with my request in the sense that there was no mention of the quality of my work and my conduct in the exercise of my official functions. I requested him to send me a certificate in accordance with Article 1095 of the Staff Regulations.

On September 28th, 2009, Mr. Antoine Mouzinga sent me an email informing me to contact the Secretary of the Appeals

Committee for the Appeal Procedures of the Decision of the WHO Regional Director. Mr. Mouzinga returned to me attached the same certificate.

Despite 4 other calls (October 5, October 14, October 27 and November 6, 2009), I still remain, to this day, without a certificate.

Seeing that the administration was not acting in good faith in its conduct towards me, I sent a request for review of the decision to terminate my employment to the Regional Director on October 11 2009.

It is clear that the decision not to renew my appointment could only have been taken after September 1st, 2008 since on that date and following the guidance of the Regional Director my name was added to the list of participants in the awareness and training workshop on GSM in Gaborone.

If not, how can they explain my participation in a GSM workshop scheduled to be launched on November 1st, 2008, 4 days before the end of my contract? If the decision not to renew my appointment had been made before September 1st, 2008, the administration would have sent someone other than me to this workshop. Common sense dictates that you do not train someone who will not even have time to implement what they have learned. Please note that my participation in this workshop cost more than twenty-five thousand (US$25,000).

The decision not to renew my temporary appointment was made after October 20th, 2008, the date on which the administration received the falsified documents that my superior had made available to them.

The administration's exercise of its discretionary power not to renew my appointment is, therefore, vitiated by the abuse of power by my superior. This is, without a doubt, a misuse by the Administration of its discretionary power to which the United Nations Administrative Tribunal referred in its judgment No. 885.

There is no doubt, in light of the facts set out above, that the exercise by the administration of its discretionary power not to extend my appointment was affected by the violation of the principle of good faith in dealings with civil servants, bias, arbitrariness, and abuse of power. Time limits for appealing a final decision of the Administration.

Aware that the argument of discretionary power was not consistent in the case before us because the decision not to renew my appointment was vitiated by abuses of power (arbitrariness, irregularity of procedure, irregularity of motivation, and other extrinsic motivations), the administration suggests that my appeal is inadmissible under Article 1230.8.3 of the Staff Regulations.

It is surprising that the administration is now bringing up the notion of time limits to argue the inadmissibility of my appeal, especially when we know the Administration's behavior in this area. If there is any delay, it is because the Administration wanted it to be that way.

I clearly informed the administration on November 5th, 2008, the day I received the decision not to renew my appointment, that I was going to contest the "evaluation report" of my hierarchical superior.

I subsequently informed the Administration on numerous occasions of my intention to appeal the decision. At no time did the administration mention the time limits for appeal or the need to contact the Regional Appeals Committee.

The deadlines of Article 1230.8.3 of the Staff Regulations assume that the Administration acts in good faith, which was not the case at all. Dr sambo in his December 13, 2008, told Mr. Durao verbatim, "RPO Penso que se deve ouvir o impetrante. Saudacoes." Translation: "I think the petitioner should be heard. Greetings."

Mr. Durao had asked me for my telephone number and promised to call me; Which he never did.

If Mr. Durao did not want to discuss the matter as the Regional Director suggested, he only had to provide me with a copy of the rules and procedures of the Regional Appeals Committee so that I could avail myself of them. Mr. Durao had done none of that.

Even when I asked for a copy of the rules and procedures of the Regional Appeals Committee, Mr. Durao sent me a copy of the part of the Staff Regulations and Rules concerning appeals committees.

In addition to the administration's behavior in this matter, I was called upon to leave Mali and return to Canada.

The Regional Appeals Committee will have to take all these facts into consideration when deciding on the admissibility of the appeal.

Montreal February 10, 2010

Nour-Eddine Benakezouh, MBA
yassirem@yahoo.com

The Regional Appeals Committee (RAC) submitted its report to the Regional Director on March 30th, 2020.

If compliance with WHO rules and regulations is the least of the concerns of the Regional Office, the RAC does not care about them at all. This non-compliance is evident in the report the RAC submitted to the Regional Director.

In addition to not caring about the regulations, of which The RAC members have only a vague knowledge, lying seems to be at the root of their actions.

The lies started very early in their report. Indeed, in the first paragraph of their report it is clearly written:

- *"At the request of the applicant, the appeal was examined behind closed doors, on the basis of the written documentation provided."*

Contrary to what was written in the report, at no time did I ask that the appeal to be examined behind closed doors. I did not even know that I had this option since the regional office and the RAC were stingy with information regarding the appeal procedures. I was forced to play dentist to extract from them the little information on the appeal procedures that I was able to extract from.

The RAC does not limit itself to non-compliance with regulations; it extends its lack of respect to individuals. In fact, the committee did not even bother to spell my first and last name correctly. In their report, I became **Noor-Eddine Benekezouh** instead of **Nour-Eddine Benakezouh.**

Five people supposedly read the report before signing it. No one has noticed that my last and first names were misspelled. This is formal proof of the seriousness with which the members of the RAC fulfilled their obligations. Unfortunately, this is not the only anomaly. Anomalies that made the report not worth the ink with which it was printed.

I have no other choice than to translate the RAC report from French to English so the reader can see for himself the full extent of the anomalies contained in that report. I will then highlight every anomaly.

"AFRO REGIONAL APPEAL COMMITTEE

APPEL No. RAC/006/2010

M. NOOR-EDDINE BENEKEZOUH

Report to the Regional Director

Committee Members

> Mr. Marc Bigot, 2nd substitute,
> Mr. Jules Bekombo, 2nd substitute representative of the R-D
> Mr. Pascal Mouhouelo, representative of the staff association,
> Mrs. Angèle Mandzoungou, Secretary, RAC,
> Ms. Claudine Murerwa, Secretary, Regional Appeal Committee.

Meeting dates and procedures

1. The AFRO Regional Appeals Committee (hereinafter, the RAC) met on March 25th, 2010 to examine the appeal submitted on January 28th, 2010 by the applicant. The latter contests the decision of the Regional Personnel Administration officer notified by a memorandum dated () November 5th, 2008 for the non-extension of the temporary contract. At the request of the applicant, the appeal was examined in camera, on the basis of the written documentation provided.

The subject of the Appeal

2. *The applicant was an AFRO staff member in the Mali country office. He joined WHO on November 10th, 2007, for an initial period of 11 months as an Administration officer in the WHO Mali office.*

3. *The applicant contests the decision of November 5th, 2008 contained in a memorandum from RPO that he received concerning the non-extension of the temporary contract.*

Admissibility

5. *The RAC noted that the appeal was not submitted within the time limits provided for in Article 1230.8.3 of the Staff Regulations and Article 1040 of the Staff Regulations and the Staff Regulations on the "end of appointments". The appellant should intervene no later than 60 calendar days following the date of actual receipt of notification of the decision. There was an exchange on the December 13th, December 15th, 2008, and January 29th, 2009 emails, to request the missing annexes and certificate of service. However, Mr. Benakezouh waited more than a year to submit his appeal.*

Chronology

November 10, 2007- November 9, 2008 –

The Applicant's appointment with WHO as international temporary staff for a period of 12 months.

November 5, 2008-

Notification of non-extension of the temporary contract, in accordance with Article 1040 of the Staff Regulations.

November 6, 2008 –

An extension of the contract for one month was extended for Mr. Benakezouh, who was hired on a temporary basis.

Position of the Applicant

6. *Following the version of events formulated by the Administration (RPO memorandum of November 5, 2008).*

Position of the Administration

7. *The Administration bases its response on Article 1230.8.3 of the Staff Regulations that the deadline was not respected.*

Considerations of the Appeal Committee

8. *The Committee had set itself the task of verifying firstly: Article 1230.8.3 of the Staff Regulations, and Article 540 paragraph 540.1.3 of the Staff Regulations and the Staff Regulations on the "end of engagements," confirm the inadmissibility of the appeal.*

Conclusions of the Appeal Committee

9. *The RAC examined the applicant's various correspondence.*

   9.1 He considered that the applicant had not respected the deadline for submitting an appeal.

   9.2 He notes that the reasons given by Mr. Benakezouh in support of his appeal against the decision not to extend his temporary contract are null and void.

Recommendations of the Appeal Committee

10. The Appeals Committee confirms the inadmissibility of the appeal submitted by Mr. Benakezouh.

A quick reading of the report of the Regional Appeals Committee (CRA) highlights the other anomalies that I listed in my correspondence of April 9, 2010 to the Regional Director of the WHO.

Instead of looking for articles of regulations to reach a decision, the members of the RAC did everything they could to find an article or a judgement to justify a decision they had already made. Instead of focusing on finding a cure for a disease, they spent their time finding a disease for a cure they already had.

Since they could find any of these, they appealed to articles that had nothing to do with the case before and that contradicted their decision.

If the members of the RAC were interested in reaching a decision, they could have resorted to all the judgments of the U N Administrative Tribunal in similar cases. Judgments in which WHO was a defendant.

Since the objective of the RAC members was far from ensuring compliance with rules and regulations, they turned a blind eye to the abuse of power, the misuse by the Administration of its discretionary power to refuse to renew a contract, the capriciousness of bias, the falsehoods and the serious breach of due process guarantees.

Very well served by the RAC which sowed well, the regional Director had no problem harvesting what turned out to be an excellent harvest for the regional office.

In his April 9th 2010 correspondence addressed to me, Dr Sambo went so far as to state the following:

Modern Day Slavery

"I have carefully examined the report and have taken due note of the conclusions and recommendations of the RAC."

I have no choice but to let you read the correspondence from the WHO Regional Director before listing the anomalies contained in the CRA report which served as a springboard for the Regional Director's.

World Health Organization
Regional Bureau for Africa
Cité du Djoué P.O Box 06, , Brazzaville,
Republic of Congo
Tel: (+(47241) 39100/ + (242) 770.02.02
Fax REG: +(47241) 39503)

Date: 09 April 2010

M. Nour-Eddine Benakezouh,

Confidential

Dear Mr. Benakezouh,

I inform you that I have received the Regional Appeals Committee (RAC) report, relating to the appeal that you filed on January 25, 2010. You will find attached a copy of said report.

I have carefully examined the report and have taken careful note of the RAC's conclusions and recommendations.

The RAC's conclusions show the following:

1. *The inadmissibility of the applicant's appeal due to the notification of the application outside the statutory time limit,*

2. *The reasons you give in support of your appeal of the decision not to renew your temporary contract are null and void.*

In view of the above, the Committee recommends that you be notified of the inadmissibility of your appeal.

Therefore, I have decided to follow the recommendations of the RAC and reject your appeal against the Administration of the WHO AFRO Regional Office.

My decision is final. I hope that you will accept it. Otherwise, in accordance with the provisions of Staff Regulation 1230.8.5, you have the right to appeal my decision to the Headquarters Board of Appeal. Notification of this appeal must be sent in writing to the Headquarters Board of Appeal within a maximum period of sixty (60) calendar days from the date of receipt of this letter.

Please accept, Dear Sir, the expression of my best regards.

Dr. Luis G. Sambo
Regional Director

P.J.: As mentioned
cc: President RAC"

The Director conducted such a thorough review of the CRA report that he missed all of the anomalies in the report:

1. My name is **Nour-Eddine Benakezouh** and not **Noor-Eddine Benekezouh.**
2. I joined WHO on November 9 2007 and not on November 10 2007 as stated in paragraph 2 of the RAC report.
3. I joined WHO for an initial period of 12 months and not 11 months as stipulated in paragraph 2 of the RAC report.

4. The RAC report does not contain a paragraph 4. The RAC members moved from paragraph 3 to paragraph 5.

5. The email exchanges on the 13th and the 15th of December 2008 had nothing to do with the claim for missing annexes and certificate of service, as supported in paragraph 5 of the RAC report.

6. There was no email on January 29, 2009, in my request, contrary to what is written in paragraph 5 of the RAC report.

7. Article 1040 of the Staff Regulations and Staff Rules does not, in any way, shape or form, concern time limits for appeals and, therefore, does not provide for any provision concerning the latter, contrary to what is stated by the RAC in paragraph 5 of its report to the Regional Director to confirm the inadmissibility of the appeal.

8. The extension of my contract took place on November 5, 2008, and not December 6, 2008, as mentioned in the chronology section of the RAC report.

9. My contract was extended by exactly 26 days (November 10th to December 5th, 2008) and not by one month as the wording in the timeline section suggests.

10. The applicant's position (paragraph 6) is incomprehensible.

11. Paragraph 540.1.3 of the Staff Regulations and Staff Rules does not concern the **"end of appointments"** as written in paragraph 8 of the RAC report but rather the **"end of the probationary period."** I do not see, therefore, how paragraph 540.1.3 of Article 540 can confirm the inadmissibility of my appeal.

12. Even if we accept that Article 540 can apply to my case, the Regional Appeal Committee should have read the sub-article 540.2. Since 540.2 is in total contradiction with their decision, they chose to stop reading the staff regulations and staff rules less than one inch from where the sub-article 540.2 begins.

The Director has examined the RAC report so carefully that he has overlooked all the anomalies in the report.

If the Regional Director's behavior does not amount to contempt, I really don't know what behavior could qualify as such.

In fact, despite all these anomalies and irregularities, the Regional Director decided, as he mentioned in his letter of April 9th, 2010, to *"follow the recommendations of the RAC and reject your appeal against the Administration of the WHO AFRO Regional Office."*

I will never understand how the Director General can accept recommendations from the RAC that are based on an inappropriate article of regulation. Indeed, article 540 of the staff regulations and staff status concerns, as its name indicates, the end of the probationary period.

540. END OF PROBATION

540.1 A performance evaluation report (see Rule 530.2) shall be made before the end of the normal probationary period (see Rule 420.7). On the basis of this report, a decision shall be taken and notified to the staff member that the:

540.1.1. appointment is confirmed;

> 540.1.2. probationary period is extended for a specified period;
>
> 540.1.3 The appointment is not confirmed."

Having had the solemn confirmation that the WHO regional management for Africa did not want to hear about modern-day slavery, which has become a taboo subject, because talking about this subject would inevitably lead them to ask themselves the question of who protects Dr. Diallo, I had come to the conclusion that it was naive of me to believe for a second that Dr Sambo was going to put an end to an injustice that had lasted too long since putting an end to this injustice would require his incrimination and I weigh carefully my words carefully.

My new mindset certainly did not mean that I was going to give up. On the contrary, the Regional Director's decision confirmed for me all the information that I had and I needed to confirm: Dr Sambo found himself in a conflict-of-interest situation. In fact, he was a player and a referee in a game that lasted too long.

To put an end to this misery, I decided to exercise my right to appeal the regional director's decision to the Headquarters Board of Appeal with the hope that somebody will see the light of day.

M. Nour-Eddine Benakezouh, MBA
yassirem@yahoo.com

May 10th, 2010

Mrs. Isabelle Micheloni,
Headquarters Appeals Committee,
World Health Organization.
Object: Appeal Brief (Cas No. 755)

Dear Mrs. Micheloni,

In accordance with Article I of the internal regulations of the Appeals Committee of the Seat, I respectfully submit my brief under the conditions set out in Article 12 of the same regulations.

In accordance with Rule 13 of the Rules of Procedure of the Headquarters Board of Appeal, I have sent a copy of my submission to the Regional Director of the African Region of the World Health Organization since it is an appeal under Rule 4 against a decision of the Regional Director.

Pending a favorable response to my present request, I ask the members of the Regional Committee of the Headquarters to accept my distinguished greetings and remain at your entire disposal for any information or document that you may need for the evaluation of my request.

Nour E. Benakezouh

Modern Day Slavery

MEMORANDUM OF APPEAL OF THE DECISIONOF THE REGIONAL DIRECTOR

Table of Contents

Section I. Procedures 158

Section II. Timeline of events.. 159

Section III. Position of the Applicant 172

Section IV. Recovery 193

Section V. Examination Method & Committee composition 197

Section VI. LISTE OF ANNEXES 198

Section 1. Procedures

M. Nour-Eddine Benakezouh
yassirem@yahoo.com

Details of the decision against which the applicant wishes to appeal:

The decision of the Regional Director in his letter of April 9, 2010, informing me that he rejects my appeal, agreeing with the RAC that:

1. My appeal was not admissible; and
2. The reasons given in support of my appeal of the decision not to renew my temporary contract are null and void.

Grounds for the appeal (Staff Regulation 1230.1)

1. Article 1230.1.1: bias shown by a superior or by any other official involved in the decision in question;
2. Article 1230.1.2; incomplete examination of the facts;
3. Article 1230.1.3: non-observance or unfounded application of the provisions of the Staff Regulations, the Staff Regulations, or the terms of his contract.

I, Nour-Eddine Benakezouh, declare that I have exhausted all existing administrative channels provided for in Article 1230.8.1 of the Staff Regulations.

10-05-2010

Modern Day Slavery

Nour-Eddine Benakezouh

Section 2. Timeline of events

1. I joined the WHO Representation Office in Mali on November 9, 2007 as an administration officer, under a temporary appointment for a period of one year (A1).

2. On January 25, 2008, during the first meeting I had with my superior, Dr. Fatoumata Binta Diallo, I raised the issue of my activity plan (Section A of the PMDS form) (A2).

3. Being new to the organization and having officials to evaluate, I had brought to the attention of my superior that the evaluation of the staff was the area where I needed the most support. I also brought to her attention the fact that I still did not have a job description as an administration officer.

4. I verbally raised the issue of my business plan with my superior several times (once a month).

5. On July 10th, 2008, the same day of my medical evacuation to Paris, France, after 6 nights of hospitalization at the Pasteur Clinic in Bamako, Mali, where I was treated with morphine to alleviate unbearable pain, my superior summoned me to a meeting asking me to fill out part A (Activity Plan) of the PMDS form.

6. Despite my health condition, the fact that I am participating in this process for the first time, and the absence of a job description, I listed four objectives that I had to carry out during the evaluation period with the hope of improving them during the meeting with my superior and went to her Office.

7. My superior was not ready to fill out my activity plan. I think she did not think that I would respond positively to her summons given my health condition. She spoke to me in

generalities even when I reminded her that this was my first year at WHO and that I needed all her help.

8. All what my superior had communicated to me during our meeting, that lasted less than 10 minutes, was to make my objectives S M A R T without any other explanation.

9. On August 26, 2008, Ms. Marie Louise Omog sent an email (A3) to the Country Office Representatives and Administration officers containing the attached list of participants in the GSM awareness and training workshop in Gaborone, Botswana (18-22 September 2008). **My name was on this list.**

10. The great importance of the GSM awareness and training workshop, the implementation of which will completely change the way WHO Country Offices operate, is explained in the email (A4) of August 29 2008 from Mr. Andres Nzang.

11. The launch of GSM in the WHO African Region was scheduled for November 1, 2008 (4 days before the end of my temporary appointment and 25 days after the date on which the Administration was to notify me of the non-renewal of my appointment in the event that my appointment was not to be renewed).

12. On August 29 2008, following the intervention of my superior at the Regional Office, Mrs. Marie Louise Omog sent an email (A5) to the Representatives and Administration officers of the Country Offices containing as an attachment the list of participants in the GSM awareness and training workshop in Gaborone. **My name vanished from the list.**

13. The same day, I sent an email (A6) to Dr Oladapo Walker informing him that my name was no longer on the August 29th list.

14. On August 30th, 2008, I sent another email (A7) to Ms. Marie Louise Omog asking her why I was the only administration officer in Africa whose name did not appear on the August 29th list.

15. On September 1st, 2008, Mr. Andres Nzang sent an email (A8) to the Country Office Representatives and Administration officers containing the attached final list of participants in the GSM awareness and training workshop in Gaborone. **My name was put back on the list**.

16. In this email, Mr. Andres Nzang had clearly written, "Following the guidance of the Regional Director, please find attached the final list of participants in the workshop mentioned in the subject line."

17. Not content with my name being put back on the final list of participants in the GSM awareness and training workshop in Gaborone, my superior spent the next fortnight taking steps with the Regional Office to prevent me from participating in this workshop and, thereby, destroying my chances of having my appointment renewed since she had already unilaterally decided to terminate my appointment.

18. The September 11th, 2008 email (A9) (11 days after receipt of the memo from Mr. Andres Nzang) from my superior is irrefutable proof of my superior's relentlessness and her desire to remove me from this workshop and, therefore, to terminate my engagement.

19. I finally attended the GSM awareness and training workshop in Gaborone, after the intervention of the Regional Director.

20. On October 2nd, 2008, my superior sent an email (A10) to all civil servants with the subject line: PMDS review. My superior did not mention in this email, at any time, my refusal to be evaluated. On the contrary, she stated that I was on the list of civil servants she had already met. She also stated that she had analyzed the civil servants' documents, and her comments are available.

21. On Monday, October 6th, 2008, after a radio silence of almost 3 months (July 10 to October 6, 2008), my superior sent me an email (A11) informing me that she expected my documents no later than Tuesday, October 7th before 12:00. In her email, she made a statement that was completely contradictory to the one she had made four days earlier.

22. On Tuesday, October 7th, 2008, I went to my superior's Office four times. I had the opportunity to be received by my superior very early in the morning (7:30). I explained to her that I had prepared Part A (Activity Plan) of my PMDS but that I could not access it because of the problem we had with the computer network. My superior had asked me to do it during the day.

23. Once the computer network was restored (around 10 a.m.), I printed a copy of Part A of my PMDS and went to my superior's Office twice during the morning. My superior could not see me, claiming a busy schedule. I asked Mrs. Aoua Dembélé, my secretary, who was replacing my superior's secretary, to let me know as soon as I could be seen.

24. Having received no sign from Mrs. Aoua Dembélé, I went to my superior's Office for the fourth time at the end of the working day. Mrs. Dembélé, after consulting with my superior, came back to tell me that Dr. Diallo was asking me to come back the next day, although, in her email of the previous day, she clearly stated that she was expecting the documents on Tuesday before 12:00 and that I had to go, as well as my superior and a large part of the Office's employees, the following 2 days (Wednesday October 8th and Thursday, October 9th, 2008) to the UNDAF Global Task Force meeting which was being held outside the WHO office and which was going to last two full days.

25. The high importance of this meeting is underlined by my superior in her October 7th, 2008 (A12) and October 8th, 2008 (A13) emails sent to all officials in which she postponed the meeting of officials from Thursday October 9th to Monday October 13th, 2008.

26. October 10th, 2008 (one month before the end of my contract) is the date on which the Administration was to notify me of the non-renewal of my contract in the event that my contract was not renewed (article 1040.1 of the Staff Regulations and Rules).

27. On Friday, October 10th, 2008, at 14:02 (the WHO representation office in Mali closes at 12:00 on Fridays, and the organizing Committee of the Global Ministerial Forum on Research for Health of which I was a member met at 15:00 every Friday), my superior sent an email (A14) to Mr. Haarman, Director of Administration and Finance, with copies to Mr. Durao, Regional Personnel Administration officer, to Mr. Wadda and to myself, telling him that I was

unable to send her my PMDS and that she was going to send him her evaluation unilaterally.

28. On the same day, my superior sent another email (A15) to Mr. Haarman with copies to Mr. Durao and Mr. Wadda asking them to: "note that the start date of Mr. Nour's contract is November 9th, 2007 instead of the 14th." My superior did not send me a copy of this email.

29. On October 11th, 2008, Mr. Haarman sent an email (A16) to my superior and to Mr. Durao, with a copy to Mr. Wadda, in which he said, "This is noted, and we will therefore study your evaluation report upon receipt. Please do not forget to copy the person concerned." Although Mr. Haarman asked my superior not to forget to copy me, she did not copy me in her email.

30. On Monday, October 13th, 2008, as soon as I became aware of the email of October 10th, I sent an email (A17) to Mr. Haarman and my superior, with copies to Mr. Durao and Mr. Wadda, expressing my availability to be evaluated because, "**one of my tasks within the WHO Representation Office in Mali is to ensure compliance with the rules and regulations of the organization. The PMDS is an integral part of these, and I am aware that I must, therefore, set an example in this area, especially since the process provides for a system of appeal if I were to question the objectivity of my evaluation.**"

31. On October 14th, 2008, my superior sent to Mr. Haarman and Mr. Durao, with copies to Mr. Wadda and myself, an email (A18) including, as an attachment, her unilateral "Evaluation Report" (A 19) completely ignoring the fact that I had stated to her in writing on October 13th that I was

ready to be evaluated. Please note that the "Evaluation Report" was not signed by my superior.

32. On October 15, 2008, I sent an email (A20) to my superior, Mr. Haarman, and Mr. Durao, with a copy to Mr. Wadda acknowledging receipt of the "Evaluation Report" and promising a response to my superior's allegations by Monday, October 20 "if I have received the annexes by then."

33. On October 20th, 2008, my superior sent the annexes of her unilateral "evaluation report" to Mr. Haarman and Mr. Durao, refusing to give me a copy of these annexes despite my request, made in the email of October 15th.

34. On 22 October 2008, I sent an email (A 21) to Mr. Haarman and Mr. Durao, with copies to my supervisor and Mr. Wadda, apologizing for not having sent my response to my supervisor's allegations because I had still not received a copy of the annexes to her "evaluation report".

35. Seeing nothing coming, I called Mr. Haarman on October 25th, 2008, and left a message in his voicemail informing him that I had still not received the annexes and could, therefore, not adequately respond to the allegations of my hierarchical superior.

36. On October 27th, 2008, Mr. Haarman sent an email (A22) to my superior asking her to "give me a copy as soon as possible in accordance with the regulations and practices in this type of situation." Please note that, instead of playing that game, Mr. Haarman could have sent me a copy of those annexes since Dr. Diallo sent him a copy of them.

37. On November 3rd, 2008, my superior finally gave me a copy of the annexes in question. My first surprise was to see that the annexes were not numbered. My second was to discover that my superior had not given me all the annexes that she had sent to the Regional Office.

38. On November 5th, 2008, when I was finishing my responses to the allegations made by my superior, the Regional Personnel Administration Officer sent me, through the latter, a memorandum informing me of the decision not to renew my appointment (A23) and a memorandum of the formalities for ending appointments (A24).

39. The administration did not provide me with the reasons for its decision not to renew my appointment, and the administration's notice was late.

40. The same day I called Mr. Durao on the phone several times to get explanations concerning the end-of-engagement memorandum (late notice, no reasons for the decision, etc.). I left four messages in his voicemail asking him to contact me. Since I did not receive any replies to my messages, I then sent him an email (A25) the same day.

41. Faced with Mr. Durao's silence, I telephoned Mr. Charlemagne Pissara, compliance officer at the regional office, on November 7th, 2008, to ask him for advice on how to behave in the face of Mr. Durao's silence. Mr. Pissara had asked me to give him some time to make inquiries.

42. An hour later, Mr. Charlemagne sent me an email (A26) in which he asked me: "try again to contact Mr. Durao who is the "Personnel Officer" for the course of action to take given

that you have already sent him a memorandum. At this stage my intervention would be inappropriate."

43. On November 19th, 2008, just two weeks after deciding not to renew my appointment, the Administration proceeded to appoint a new administration officer despite the fact that I had informed Mr. Durao of my concerns regarding the decision not to renew my contract and that the time limits for appealing had not expired.

44. The speed at which the administration proceeded with the appointment of the new administration officer is clear proof of the administration's bias and its desire to deprive me of my right to due process. To be convinced of this, it is enough to know that the administration officer position of the WHO Representation Office in Mali remained vacant for almost two years before my appointment. The Administration, by proceeding so quickly with my replacement, wanted to present me with a fait accompli, especially since it was informed of my decision to contest the decision not to renew my appointment.

45. On December 13th, 2008, I sent an email (A27) to Mr. Durao, with copies to Mr. Durao with Copies to Mr. Haarman, Dr Luis Gomes Sambo, WHO Regional Director, the Director-General of WHO and Dr. Diallo in which I clearly denounced the abuse of power by my superior (lies, half-truths and falsification of documents) and my intention to object to my superior's "evaluation report."

46. On the same day, Dr Sambo, WHO Regional Director, sent an email (A28) to Mr. Durao and me with a copy to Mr. Haarman, in which he said verbatim in Portuguese to Mr. Durao, "RPO Penso que se deve ouvir o impetrante.

Saudacoes." Translation: "RPO, I think we should hear the petitioner. Greetings."

47. On December 15th, 2008, Mr. Durao sent me an email (A29) apologizing for the silence and asking me to give him a telephone number where he could reach me.

48. The same day, I responded to this email (A29) by providing my telephone numbers in Montreal since I had to leave Bamako that day to return home to Montreal.

49. I sent an email on January 18th, 2009 (A30) to Mr. Durao, with a copy to Mr. Haarman, asking him to send me a copy of the annexes submitted by my superior with her "Evaluation Report" since my legal advisor, like me, suspected that certain annexes were missing. The fact that my superior had not numbered the annexes complicated matters considerably. My legal advisor suggested that I obtain a copy of all the annexes to avoid any further surprises once I would be before the United Nations Administrative Tribunal.

50. On January 26th, 2008, I sent another email (A31) to Mr. Durao reminding him that I had still not received a response from him despite all his promises and reiterating my intention and willingness to do everything humanly possible to maintain my reputation and dignity.

51. On January 27th, 2008, Mr. Durao sent me an email (A32) informing me that he would send me the documents that I had requested.

52. On January 29th, 2009, Mr. Éric Tagnon, on Mr. Durao's instructions, sent me an email (A32) to which he attached the annexes I had requested. A check of these annexes confirmed that some annexes were indeed missing from the documents

that Dr. Diallo sent me two months earlier. I understood at that time why the annexes were not numbered and why my superior had refused to give them to me initially and then only gave me part of them when Mr. Haarman insisted that she should give me a copy of those documents. In fact, my superior had submitted falsified documents.

53. It took 5 emails (November 5th, 2008, December 13th and 15th, 2008, January 18th and 26th, 2009) and a wait of more than 3 months (October 14th, 2008 to January 29th, 2009) to receive the entire file of the "evaluation report" from my hierarchical superior.

54. The administration, despite Mr. Durao's apologies and promises to call me to discuss my concerns and objections to the decision not to renew my appointment, made no effort to get my version of the facts. Even my allegations of falsification of documents by my superior did not seem to concern the administration. I do not think there could be better proof of arbitrariness and bias on the part of the administration.

55. All my efforts to find out the reasons for the non-renewal of my appointment were met with the refusal to cooperate of the administration, which refused to respond to my voice messages and emails despite the instructions of the Regional Director and the promises of Mr. Durao.

56. Having received no call from Mr. Durao, contrary to what he had promised me in his December 15th, 2008 email and noticing that the administration was not paying any consideration to my efforts, I sent an email (A33) to Mr. Durao on September 13th, 2009, reminding him that I was

still waiting for his phone call and my determination to see this matter through to the end.

57. *I had also asked Mr. Durao, in the same email, to send me a certificate concerning the nature of my duties, the duration of my services, the quality of my work, and my conduct in the exercise of my official functions in accordance with Article 1095 (A34) of the Staff Regulations and Rules in order to submit it to the organizations that had requested it as part of the evaluation of my application, as well as a copy of the procedure(s) for appealing the decision of the Regional Director.*

58. *On September 18th, 2009, Mr. Wadda sent me an email (A35) with an attached certificate (A 36). Please note that for reasons that I still do not know, Mr. Wadda did not finish his sentence in which he tried to give the conditions for extending my commitment.*

59. *On September 23rd, 2009, Mr. Durao sent me a copy of the part of the Staff Regulations and Rules concerning appeal committees and not the rules and procedures of the Regional Appeal Committee.*

60. *On September 24th, 2009, I had sent an email to Mr. Durao (A37) informing him that the certificate sent to me was not in accordance with my request in the sense that there was no mention of the quality of my work and my conduct in the exercise of my official functions. I requested him to send me a certificate in accordance with Article 1095 of the Staff Regulations and Rules.*

61. *Despite 4 other emails (October 5th, October 14th and October 27th, 2009) (A38), I still remain without certificate.*

62. By refusing to send me this certificate, the administration has unfairly and illegally deprived me of an essential tool in my search for future employment since international organizations systematically ask individuals who apply for positions to present at least the latest evaluation report from a previous employer.

63. In addition to the fact that I was unable to provide an evaluation report or a certificate to the organizations that had asked me for it, UN (A39) and UNRWA (A40), I was unable to answer the question of why I had left WHO to the organizations that had asked me for it during the recruitment interviews: UNOWA (A41), UNOPS (A42), WHO (A 43) and World Bank (A44).

64. On September 28th, 2009, Mr. Antoine Mouzinga sent me an email (A45) informing me to contact the secretary of the Regional Appeals Committee for the appeal procedures of the decision of the WHO Regional Director. Mr. Mouzinga sent me back the same certificate attached.

65. The same day, I sent an email (A46) to Mrs. Mandzoungou, secretary of the Regional Appeals Committee, asking her for more information regarding the appeal procedures.

66. On September 29th, 2009, Mrs. Mandzoungou sent me an email in which she asked me to answer a series of questions (A47).

67. Given the attitude of the administration, which neither initiated discussions nor ended its proposal for discussion, and given its refusal to provide me with a certificate in accordance with Article 1095 of the Staff Regulations and Rules, I was convinced that the administration was not acting

in good faith. I then sent a request for review of the decision to terminate my appointment to the Regional Director on October 11th, 2009 (A48).

68. *On November 17th, 2009, I sent an email (A49) to Mr. Durao with copies to the Regional Director and the Director of Administration and Finance, requesting from him for the seventh time to provide me with a certificate in accordance with Article 1095 of the Staff Rules and Regulations, which was requested of me by the United Nations agencies to which I submitted my applications. Mr. Durao did not respond to any of my requests. To this day, I remain without a certificate of employment from WHO.*

69. *Having received no response to my request, I responded to the questions of the Regional Appeals Committee on November 23rd, 2009 (A50).*

70. *On December 13th, 2009, I sent an email (A51) to the Regional Appeals Committee to obtain an update on my actions since I had not received any acknowledgment of receipt and to request, once again, a copy of the procedures for appealing decisions.*

71. *On January 18th, 2010, Mrs. Mandzoungou sent me an email (A52) with, attached, a copy of the procedures.*

72. *On January 25th, 2010, I sent an email (A53) to the Regional Appeals Committee with attached a copy of my appeal brief against the decision not to extend my temporary appointment.*

73. *On January 28th, 2010, Mrs. Mandzoungou sent me an email (A54) acknowledging receipt of my appeal brief.*

74. *On February 5th, 2010, Mrs. Mandzoungou sent me an email (A55), sending me an attachment of a letter from Mr. Pule (A56), president of the RAC, and the Administration's response (A57).*

75. *The Administration stated on February 2nd, 2010, for the first time, that it did not justify its decision not to renew my contract by reasons of performance, which is true. What is even more true is the fact that the administration has still not, fifteen (18) months later, provided me with the reasons for its decision not to renew my appointment.*

76. *On February 11th, 2010, I sent an email (A59) to the Regional Appeals Committee with, attached, my response to the Administration's response (A60).*

77. *On April 9th, 2010, Mr. Eric Tagnon sent me an email (A61) with attached the letter from the Regional Director notifying me of his decision (A62) following the recommendations of the Regional Appeals Committee and a copy of the Regional Appeals Committee report (A63).*

Section 3. Position of the Applicant

78. *The WHO Regional Appeals Committee, RAC hereinafter, made errors of fact and law in its report to the WHO Regional Director when it failed to properly rule on my Appeal. To avoid any oversight or error on my part, I will list all the errors made by the RAC, although some errors are less relevant than others in this case. In citing all the errors, my aim is to demonstrate the level of professionalism demonstrated by the RAC in assessing my Appeal of the decision not to extend my appointment.*

79. My name is Nour-Eddine Benakezouh and not Noor-Eddine Benekezouh as written in the report.

80. I joined WHO on November 9, 2007, for an initial period of 12 months and not on November 10, 2007, for a period of 11 months, as stipulated in paragraph 2 of the RAC report.

81. The email exchanges on 13 and 15 December 2008 had nothing to do with the claim for missing annexes and certificate of service, as supported in paragraph 8 of the RAC report.

82. There was no email on January 29, 2009, in my request, contrary to what is written in paragraph 5 of the RAC report.

83. Article 1040 of the Staff Regulations and Staff Rules does not in any way concern appeal deadlines and therefore does not provide for any provision concerning the latter, contrary to what is stated by the Regional Appeals Committee in paragraph 5 of its report to the Regional Director to confirm the inadmissibility of the Appeal.

84. The extension of my contract took place on November 5, 2008, and not on December 6, 2008, as mentioned in the chronology section of the RAC report.

85. My contract was extended for less than one month from November 5, 2008, and not for just one month, as the wording in the timeline section suggests.

86. The applicant's position (paragraph 6) is incomprehensible.

87. Paragraph 540.1.3 of Article 540 of the Staff Regulations and Staff Rules does not concern the "end of appointments" as written in paragraph 8 of the RAC report but rather the "end of the probationary period." I do not see, therefore,

how Article 540, paragraph 540.1.3 can confirm the inadmissibility of my Appeal.

Admissibility of the Appeal

88. Article 1230.8.3 refers to the declaration of intention to appeal, which must be made within 60 calendar days following notification of the final measure to which one wishes to appeal and not to the complete declaration as the RAC maintains.

89. "According to case law, deadlines are essential to ensure the efficiency of the administration. But they are not designed as a trap that results in surprising the good faith of an applicant".

90. In its judgment, no. 1280, the ILO Administrative Tribunal stated that, "Time limits for appeals serve a legal security function. This need for security exists for both parties to the contentious relationship: for the administration, which has an interest in ensuring that the measures it is required to take cannot be indefinitely contested, and for the litigant, who must know, especially in the presence of administrative measures that go through successive stages, from the general to the specific, at what point he can act usefully, without exposing himself to the risk of seeing his Appeal rejected, either as premature or as late."

91. The regulatory provisions applicable to the WHO internal appeals system (Article 1230.8.1 of the Staff Regulations) recognize that referral to the Appeals Committee is subject to the condition that all existing "administrative appeals" have been exhausted beforehand. I was, therefore, forced to contact the administration first.

92. *According to case law, the administration must give the reasons for a decision not to renew a contract, in order to allow the civil servant to exercise his right of Appeal and the Tribunal to exercise its power of review over such a decision. These reasons may be clarified in a communication subsequent to the notification of the decision not to renew.*

93. *The fact that the administration had not justified its decision not to renew my appointment, which is in itself a serious procedural defect, also forced me to contact the administration on November 5th, 2008, by telephone, initially leaving voice messages for Mr. Durao, Regional Personnel Administration officer, and by email the same day, since I had not received a response to my voice messages, to find out the reasons for the decision not to renew my appointment and to ensure that all existing "administrative remedies" had been exhausted so that I could properly complete my appeal of the decision without worrying that my Appeal would be rejected by the Regional Appeals Committee for failure to exhaust existing "administrative remedies."*

94. *Having received no response from Mr. Durao to my communications (telephone calls and email) of November 5th, 2008, I sent an email on December 13th, 2008, to Mr. Durao announcing my determination to assert my rights.*

95. *My email of December 13th, 2008, constitutes, as far as I am concerned, my 'declaration of intention' to appeal. This declaration was made 39 days after receipt of the decision not to renew my appointment. It is, therefore, in accordance with paragraph 1230.8.3 of Article 1230 of the Staff Regulations and Staff Rules.*

96. *It is true that paragraph 1230.8.3 of Article 1230 of the Staff Regulations and Staff Rules stipulates that my declaration of intent should be addressed to the relevant committee, namely the Regional Appeals Committee. But it is also true that according to case law, the submission of an appeal to an incompetent body of an organization is sufficient to respect a deadline, the incompetent body being required to forward the Appeal in question to the competent body.*

97. *In its judgment, no. 2017, the ILO Administrative Court considered in particular that, "The submission of a document to an incompetent body of an organization is sufficient to ensure compliance with a deadline, the incompetent body being required to forward the document in question to the competent body."*

98. *According to case law, an organization must interpret the statements of an agent according to the rules of good faith; required to avoid unnecessary harm to the agent, it may also be called upon to guide him in his actions and to dispel any error.*

99. *In its judgment no. 1167, the ILO Administrative Tribunal stated, "Secondly, Article 1230.8.3, on which the decision appealed is based, does not require that the file submitted within the appeal period be complete. On the contrary, for the Appeal to be admissible, it is necessary and sufficient that the decision appealed be clearly identified and that the grounds invoked be listed."*

100. *If the administration wanted to respect the deadlines, it only had to raise this issue on December 13th, 2008, and forward my correspondence to the competent body, namely the Regional Appeals Committee.*

101. The administration should also have dispelled any risk of error in the exercise of my rights by indicating to me the avenues of appeal.

102. The administration did none of that. On the contrary, it asked for my telephone number in Canada to reach me. Something it never did.

103. In its Judgment No. 2584, the ILO Administrative Tribunal stated that: "**If an organization proposes to enter into settlement discussions, or even participates in them, good faith requires that it consider that these discussions extend the time limit for taking any other step unless it has expressly stated otherwise. Indeed, discussions aimed at reaching an amicable settlement must proceed on the assumption that no further steps will be necessary.**"

104. I contacted the administration on the day I received the decision not to renew my appointment, namely November 5th, 2008.

105. I have remained in constant contact with the administration since then for a possible resolution of the situation arising from the administration's decision not to renew my appointment, and I have never lost interest in my situation.

106. I had always acted in good faith with the administration in full compliance with the Organization's regulations and procedures. I sent a dozen letters to the administration between November 5th, 2008 and December 2nd, 2010.

107. The administration did not, at any time during this period, raise the question of the admissibility of my Appeal. It waited until February 2nd, 2010, to do so.

108. *The Regional Director's December 13th, 2008 email hinted at the possibility of a solution since it opened the door to discussions by telling Mr. Durao, the Regional Personnel Administration officer, "**I think we should hear from the petitioner.**" The petitioner, of course, was me.*

109. *Mr. Durao, who had ignored all my previous communications, followed in the footsteps of the Regional Director by sending me an email on December 15th, 2008, apologizing for his silence and justifying it. Mr. Durao had also asked me to provide him with a telephone number where he could reach me.*

110. *The question that arises is whether the correspondence of the Regional Director of December 13th, 2008 and of the Regional Personnel Administration Officer of December 15th, 2008, resulted in a suspension of the time limit within which I had to complete my notice of appeal.*

111. *Given that it was not specified in the correspondence of the Regional Director of December 13th, 2008, and the Regional Personnel Administration officer of December 15th, 2008, that the time limits within which a notice of appeal had to be completed would continue to run while the discussions were in progress, I could reasonably infer that the counter had stopped during these discussions.*

112. *Upon receipt of Mr. Durao's email, I had no reason to doubt the administration's good faith and willingness to find a solution. I wanted to exhaust all available administrative remedies. Paragraph 1230.8.1 of Staff Rule 1230 required me to do so by clearly stating, "A staff member may appeal to a committee only when all existing administrative*

remedies have been exhausted and the action that is the subject of the complaint has become final."

113. All my steps and documents show that I thought that my situation would be regularized, especially after the Regional Director December 13th, 2008 email.

114. In hindsight, I realize today that the administration was not imbued with the same faith that I had when it suggested that we discuss. The administration made no effort to reach a settlement. Mr. Durao, unlike the Regional Director, had no intention of discussing. His December 15th, 2008 email of, was simply a way of passing the time in order to exceed the deadlines within which a notice of appeal had to be completed.

115. For Mr. Durao, the delays were just a trap that resulted in surprising my good faith. If not, how can we explain the fact that Mr. Durao neither kept his promise to reach me by phone nor ended the discussions so that I could complete my appeal?

116. The Administration had been informed, orally on November 5th, 2008, and by email on December 13th, 2008, of my intention to assert my rights and restore my honor and dignity. If the administration did not intend to engage in discussions, it only had to say so at that time and answer my questions so that I could complete my Appeal.

117. The administration could have declared that the Organization would no longer follow up on my correspondence and directed me to the Regional Appeals Committee by providing me with its contact details. Contact

details that I had requested so that I could contact it, once I had exhausted all existing administrative appeals.

118. *By pretending to be interested in discussing when me, the administration demonstrated serious breaches of the principle of good faith and the duty of care incumbent on an international organization towards its officials.*

119. *It was up to the administration to either begin discussions as promised or to end them. The administration did neither. For those reasons, the administration cannot, therefore, argue today that my appeal is inadmissible.*

120. *In its Judgment No. 2066, the ILO Administrative Tribunal stated that, "The rules of good faith require that the time limit for appeal should not begin to run before an organization has taken a final decision, which is considered to be the act adversely affecting the official. With regard to the decision of January 5th, 1999, it should be recalled that, when an organization suggests to one of its officials that it is reviewing the decision it has taken with regard to him, it cannot reasonably require him to challenge that decision and the official cannot lodge an appeal against it in the absence of an express statement from the administration specifying that the procedure must continue despite the negotiations. In such a case, the case law according to which the confirmation of a previous decision does not trigger a new time limit for appeal does not apply."*

121. *In its judgment, no. 941, the ILO Administrative Court stated, "The Tribunal considers that the Organization cannot invoke its own passivity with regard to the complainant, who could legitimately think that his application was still pending*

following the dilatory response of November 12th, 1987, and who had taken all necessary steps with this in mind."

122. Faced with the passivity of the administration and the lack of good faith, despite the suggestion of the Regional Director and the promises of the Regional Personnel Administration officer, I sent a request for a review of the decision to terminate my appointment to the Regional Director on October 11th, 2009 (Appendix 36), under the provisions of Article 1230.8.2 of the Staff Regulations.

123. Having made a written request to the Regional Director concerning my engagement on October 11th, 2009, the latter is considered to have been rejected on January 11th, 2010, according to the provisions of Article 1230.8.2 of the Staff Regulations, since no response was given by the Regional Director to my request.

124. This rejection is the final decision. This rejection may, therefore, be appealed as a final measure under Article 1230.8.1. The time limit for filing a Notice of Appeal did not begin to run until January 15th, 2010, and not November 5th, 2008, as the administration claimed.

125. In light of its behavior, it would be shocking for the administration to argue today that my application is inadmissible for failure to comply with deadlines, especially when we know that the Tribunal has declared that deadlines are not designed as a trap that results in surprising the good faith of an applicant but rather a tool to ensure the efficiency of the administration.

126. Aware of the importance of respecting deadlines, the administration used them to try to trap me. After having done

everything to delay things (failure to justify the decision, refusal to respond to my communications, false promises to contact me following the request of the Regional Director, etc.), the administration is now arguing that my appeal is inadmissible for failure to respect deadlines.

127. To rule in favor of the administration by declaring my application inadmissible would be incompatible with the rules of good faith that the administration, officials, and the Tribunal must respect and would result in a shocking denial of justice.

Notice periods

128. According to consistent case law, the non-renewal of a fixed-term contract must be the subject of a decision that must be communicated to the civil servant and be based on legally founded reasons, with "reasonable notice," so as to allow him to exercise his rights, in particular that of appealing.

129. The need for a decision of non-renewal, even in the case of temporary appointment, arises upon completion of the agreed period of service. The administration's decision not to renew the appointment must be notified within the prescribed period. In the absence of notice within the time limit, the contract is implicitly renewed for a new period (see judgment 1374 (GONZALEZ, LARRANAGA, MANZANELLI, RUGERONI and TRENCHI case) of the ILO Administrative Tribunal).

130. Faced with the ambiguity of WHO Staff Rule 1040, the ILO TA, in Judgment 469, stated that: **"The Tribunal has consistently interpreted this text, as well as similar**

provisions in other organizations, to require a decision by the Director-General not to renew and notification thereof to the staff member before the prescribed date. To interpret it to mean that the appointment terminates automatically on the date of its expiry, whether or not there has been notification, would violate this rule by rendering the notification provision superfluous and would, moreover, be unreasonable and inequitable: it would mean that a staff member who, like the complainant, has been in the service of the Organization for seven years could be summarily dismissed at the end of the period. What, then, is the effect of the absence of notice? In the eyes of the Court, there can only be one, namely that the contract is implicitly renewed for a new period."

131. In its judgment 1040, the ILO Tribunal stated that, "The complainant's three-month appointment was due to end on October 9th, 1987. In accordance with his contract, he was to receive his notice of non-extension fifteen days before that date, that is to say, on September 24th, 1987. However, it was not until September 28th, 1987, that he received the notice. In these circumstances, the Tribunal considers that his appointment was extended until January 9th, 1988. **The extension of his contract by five days until October 14th, 1987, in order to complete the period of notice provided for was ineffective because the notice was late."**

132. My temporary one-year appointment was to end on November 9th, 2008. In accordance with my contract, I was to receive notice of non-extension no later than October 10th, 2008. However, it was not until November 5th, 2008, that I received the notice dated the same day. Since I did not

receive notice within the prescribed period, my appointment was implicitly renewed for another year.

Reasons for the decision not to renew an engagement

133. It is a general principle of the international civil service that any decision not to renew a fixed-term contract must be based on a good reason and that this must be communicated to the civil servant.

134. An affirmation of this principle can be found in ILO Administrative Tribunal Judgment No. 1544, which held that, *"According to the case law, which has always been consistent on this point, even if a fixed-term appointment automatically terminates on its expiry date, the official must be informed of the real reasons for the non-renewal of his contract and receive notification thereof with reasonable notice, even if the text of the contract does not expressly require it."*

135. According to the Tribunal's consistent case law, the decision not to renew a fixed-term contract is a decision that may be challenged; it must therefore comply with certain requirements. The decision must therefore be reasoned and its reasons must be communicated to the person concerned in good time, so as to enable him to exercise his rights, in particular the right to appeal, and he must be given reasonable notice.

136. Not only did the administration not provide reasons in its Memorandum of November 5th, 2008, informing me of the decision not to renew my contract, but it has also refused to provide them to me to this day despite several requests.

137. Eighteen months after being informed of the decision not to renew my contract, I still live with ignorance of the reasons for this decision despite all my efforts with the administration. This situation is not without complicating my job search since I did not have and I still do not have any answers to provide to the employers who asked me the reasons why I left my last job.

Annual assessment of civil servants' services

138. **According to case law, the examination of a civil servant's evaluation report before any decision concerning the non-renewal of his contract, is a fundamental obligation, failure to comply with which constitutes a procedural defect having the effect of leaving out an essential fact.**

139. The primary responsibility for the proper execution of the Personnel Management and Development Service (PMDS) process, including the development of a work plan, rested with my line manager. Staff Rule 530.1.1 clearly states, "Line managers shall establish a work plan in consultation with each member of staff." My line manager did not discharge this responsibility and had no intention of doing so. If not, why wait until the day before the end of my one-year temporary contract to try to do work that should have started at the beginning of the year?

140. In its judgment 2414, the ILO Administrative Tribunal stated, "*A staff member whose services are not considered satisfactory has the right to be informed in time of the complaint so that steps can be taken to remedy the situation. Furthermore, the staff member concerned is entitled to have her objectives set in advance so that she knows by what criteria her performance will henceforth be*

evaluated. These are fundamental aspects of the obligation of an international organization to act in good faith towards its staff members and to respect their dignity."

141. The fundamental considerations that lead to the conclusion that an organization must respect the rules it has laid down also imply that it cannot base a decision adversely affecting a civil servant on the fact that his work is unsatisfactory if it has not respected the rules established for evaluating that work. Nor can the decision not to convert or renew my contract be based on such a justification.

142. The Personnel Management and Development System (PMDS) is a three-step process:

    a) Establishment of activity plans based on individual objectives;

    b) Continuous feedback and dialogue on services (mid-term review); and

    c) Year-end service review.

143. My superior had not done the first two steps despite several requests from me. Since I did not establish an activity plan, my superior obviously did not do a mid-term review or a review of my services at the end of the year.

144. Aware of these shortcomings in the procedure to be followed in terms of staff evaluation in accordance with Service Note 2001/37 detailing the procedure to be followed to implement the personnel management and development system, my line manager did everything to avoid step 3 of the PMDS process (end-of-year service review). My line manager could not evaluate my professional results because my objectives were never established.

145. *My superior opted for another alternative: that of submitting a unilateral "evaluation report," which did not comply with either the letter or the spirit of the management and development of personnel services (PMDS).*

146. *My superior justified her failure to comply with WHO regulations and procedures by my refusal to be evaluated despite the fact that I had expressed, on Monday, October 13th, 2008 in an email that I sent to Mr. Sander Edward Haarman and my superior, with copies to Mr. Alvaro Durao, Mr. Alieu Wadda, my availability to be evaluated because, "one of my tasks within the WHO Representation Office in Mali is to ensure compliance with the rules and regulations of the Organization. The PMDS being an integral part of these, I am aware that I must, therefore, set an example in this matter, especially since the process provides for an appeal system if I were to question the objectivity of my evaluation."*

147. *My superior also implicitly admits in her "Evaluation report" that there were never any discussions or interviews between us about my work and no periodic report to assess my work, my conduct, and the possibilities for my development was established by my superior even though it was my first year of employment within the Organization.*

148. *The behavior of my superior constitutes a failure to comply with paragraph 530.2 of Article 530 of the Staff Regulations.*

149. *The PMDS aims, according to its user guide, "To evaluate staff in a transparent and fair manner in relation to the objectives set and to encourage them to improve themselves. There was no transparency or fairness in the Evaluation report submitted by my superior. In addition to opting for a*

unilateral evaluation," my superior also deliberately decided not to give me a copy of the annexes attached to her "Evaluation report," in complete violation of the Organization's regulations and procedures. This refusal is due to the fact that my superior had attached falsified documents as annexes to her "Evaluation report."

Incomplete examination of the facts

150. By doing so, my superior wanted to deny me the right to object to her false and defamatory allegations. In its Judgment No. 733, the United Nations Administrative Tribunal stated that, "It is a fundamental principle of law that everyone has the right to be heard in his or her case and to be given an opportunity to respond to the allegations made against him or her. By failing to provide this right, the respondent has failed in its obligation to respect due process towards the applicant."

151. The behavior of my superior in this matter is eloquent testimony to the bias shown towards me and the violation of the Organization's regulations and procedures.

152. Faced with this situation, the administration, although aware of the actions of my superior in Angola, the country where she worked before being assigned to Mali, made no effort to obtain additional information to support or refute the allegations made by my superior in her "Evaluation report." Better still, the administration did not even wait for my response before deciding not to renew my appointment.

153. My superior made very serious accusations (violent behavior, disrespect for important people, disrespectful behavior, etc.) against me in her "Evaluation report"

without any evidence. If these allegations had any basis, my superior should have provided irrefutable evidence and not resorted to falsifying documents to support her accusations.

154. Given the seriousness of my superior's accusations, the administration should have been particularly careful to respect the principle of the presumption of innocence. It should not have ignored my statements. If due process had been respected, I would have been heard before any decision was taken against me. Instead, the administration presumed that I was guilty of all of my superior's accusations and, therefore, decided not to renew my appointment.

155. The administration should have initiated disciplinary proceedings to investigate the serious allegations made by my superior and thus given me the opportunity to respond to these allegations. The fact that no disciplinary proceedings were initiated constitutes a violation of my rights and proves that the administration's decision is arbitrary and unfair. (Judgment No. 877).

156. Aware that her accusations could not bear the burden of proof, my superior preferred to play the time card. She waited until the day before the end of my contract to lay out all the accusations that common sense and good and healthy management would have wanted them to be exposed at the time of their appearance.

157. By relying solely on the unilateral "Evaluation report" of my superior to make the decision not to renew my contract, the administration conducted an incomplete examination of the facts (paragraph 1230.1.2 of Article 1230 of the Staff Regulations). The administration has, as a result, violated my rights to due process. Scrupulous and irreproachable

compliance with the procedure established by the administration is the prerequisite and indispensable condition for the proper functioning of any administrative justice system.

The discretionary power of the Administration

158. It is true that, according to case law, a staff member holding a temporary appointment is not, generally speaking, entitled to an extension. Indeed, the United Nations Administrative Tribunal has repeatedly stated that the Administration enjoys discretionary power in matters of renewal (Judgments No. 440 and No. 1003).

159. However, the established jurisprudence of the United Nations Administrative Tribunal is that the exercise of this discretionary power must not be tainted by caprice, bias, falsehood, or serious breach of due process. This discretionary power must be exercised without the intervention of any improper motivation so as to avoid an abuse of power. (Judgments 50, 109, 142, 319 and The United Nations Administrative Tribunal stated in its Judgment 885 that the exercise by the Administration of its discretionary power not to renew a contract must not be vitiated by any form of abuse of authority and that in the presence of special circumstances, in particular in the case of misuse by the Administration of its discretionary power in refusing to renew a contract, the United Nations Administrative Tribunal considered, in the same judgment, that an exception could be made to the rule of discretionary power345).

160. The United Nations Administrative Tribunal stated in its Judgment 885 that the exercise by the Administration of its

discretionary power not to renew a contract must not be vitiated by any form of abuse of authority and that in the presence of special circumstances, in particular in the case of misuse by the Administration of its discretionary power in refusing to renew a contract, the United Nations Administrative Tribunal considered, in the same judgment, that an exception could be made to the rule of discretionary power.

161. The United Nations Administrative Tribunal has also held that a staff member could, in the circumstances of the case, reasonably expect to be considered for renewal even when the non-renewal was without justification (Judgment 1254).

162. In light of the established case law of the United Nations Administrative Tribunal on contract renewal, the Administration cannot exercise its discretionary power if its decision not to renew my appointment was vitiated by any form of abuse of authority (arbitrariness, irregularity of procedure, irregularity of motivation, other extrinsic motivations).

163. I maintain that the administration's decision not to renew my temporary appointment was vitiated by the abuse of power of my superior, who submitted a unilateral "Evaluation report" riddled with lies, half-truths, and false documents, in complete violation of the Staff Regulations and Rules.

164. An analysis of the facts preceding and following the Administration's decision not to renew my appointment will show that this decision is tainted by bias, falsehoods, and a serious breach of due process. The administration cannot, therefore, rely on the rule of discretionary power to legitimize a decision vitiated by forms of abuse of power.

165. *Aware that my supervisor had violated WHO's Rules and Procedures on performance appraisal, the administration did not want to refer to my supervisor's 'Performance Appraisal Report' in its decision not to renew my appointment. To avoid any questioning of its decision not to renew my appointment, the administration, therefore, opted to use its discretionary power.*

166. *After denying me the right to respond to the false allegations made against me by my superior who made a decision based on a unilateral "Evaluation report," the Administration now wants to deprive me of my right to appeal by arguing the notion of the discretionary power of the Administration.*

167. *In its Judgment No. 826, the United Nations Administrative Tribunal stated, "Having examined the Applicant's situation, it was incumbent upon the Respondent to make a decision in accordance with due process. Since the Applicant's performance assessment was a relevant factor, it is unacceptable that her future was decided before the rebuttal procedure had been completed. The Tribunal finds unreasonable the Department of Public Information's argument that the outcome of the rebuttal procedure had no bearing on its decision not to renew the Applicant's appointment. To accept this proposition would render the entire rebuttal procedure instituted by the Organization meaningless."*

Reintegration

168. *Consistent case law shows that a service contract, even if it is of fixed term, has the effect of creating a public law employment relationship inserted in a statutory and administrative context from which requirements or*

consequences may arise that go beyond the framework of the contractual relationship itself. Thus, reinstatement may be considered, even in the case of a fixed-term contract, in exceptional situations, when an organization systematically uses such contracts to deal with permanent administrative tasks, when a contractual relationship has been vitiated by unacceptable administrative practices, or when the untimely non-renewal of a contract has the effect of depriving an employee of his or her pension rights.

169. The WHO African Region systematically uses fixed-term contracts to deal with permanent administrative tasks. The position of Administration officer that I held at the WHO Representation in Mali is a position that has always existed, and the administrative tasks of this position are permanent, although the contracts offered to administration officers are fixed-term contracts.

170. The contractual relationship I had with WHO was vitiated by unacceptable administrative practices set out above. It is, therefore, legitimate, in light of the sequence of administrative actions recalled in detail above, to consider reinstatement to my position as Administration officer.

Section 4. Recovery

171. I respectfully request the Headquarters Appeals Committee to state that the Administration's decision not to offer me an extension of my temporary contract is the result.

172. *I respectfully request the Appeals Committee of the Seat to state that:*

   a. *The WHO Regional Appeals Committee made errors of fact and law in its report to the WHO Regional Director when it confirmed in its report that my Appeal against the decision not to renew my contract is inadmissible for failure to comply with the time limits;*

   b. *The administration has breached WHO regulations and failed to comply with the obligations arising from case law regarding the period of notice in the event of non-renewal of a contract and that my temporary employment contract has been implicitly renewed for a further period of twelve months until November 9th, 2009;*

   c. *The extension of my contract by twenty-six days, until December 5th, 2008, by the administration in order to complete the period provided for in the notice period was ineffective because the notice was late;*

   d. *In the absence of a valid decision terminating my appointment, the contractual relations between me and WHO continue, and I am entitled to benefits from the latter since the date on which WHO terminated my appointment (December 5th, 2008);*

   e. *A new decision on whether or not to renew my contract could only be taken in compliance with the procedural and substantive rules that govern it:*

   f. *The administration had an obligation to provide reasons for the decision not to renew my contract, and by not providing the reasons for the non-renewal of my appointment, the administration demonstrated serious breaches of the regulations, the requirements of the law, the principle of good faith and the duty of care incumbent on an international organization towards its officials;*

g. *The refusal to provide me with the reasons for the non-renewal of my appointment, despite several requests, constitutes an abuse of power;*

h. *The administration had a contractual obligation to carry out an annual evaluation of my work in accordance with the regulations and procedures in force;*

i. *The unilateral "Evaluation report" of my services prepared by my hierarchical superior does not comply with the provisions governing the preparation of evaluation reports for civil servants. It is also incompatible, both in substance and in procedure, with the aims and objectives of the Personnel Management and Development System (PMDS);*

j. *The process of my evaluation took place under conditions that seriously violated my rights to a fair trial;*

k. *The examination of my evaluation report before taking the decision concerning the non-renewal of my contract is a fundamental obligation, the non-compliance of which constitutes a procedural defect;*

l. *The Administration's failure to conduct an evaluation of my work, in accordance with the Organization's regulations and procedures, before deciding not to renew my appointment constitutes a violation of the procedure in force and of my conditions of employment;*

m. *The unilateral "Evaluation report" of my services prepared by my superior was inextricably linked to the decision not to renew my appointment;*

n. *The Administration, following pressure from my superior, seriously violated my right to due process when it investigated and settled the case that resulted in the non-renewal of my appointment by denying me the right to respond to the false and defamatory allegations made by my superior;*

o. *The decision not to renew my contract, made on November 5th, 2008, was tainted, in particular, because of the haste with which it was taken, by various defects with regard to the requirements of fundamental rights of civil servants;*

p. *The violation of established procedures led to the irregular exercise by the Administration of its discretionary power not to renew my appointment;*

q. *The Administration, by taking the decision not to renew my contract, caused me certain material harm and made me suffer moral harm which must be repaired;*

r. *I was deprived of my hope of a renewal of my engagement and thereby lost an opportunity to increase the length of my services;*

s. *The Administration, by refusing to provide me with a certificate, in accordance with Article 1095 of the Staff Regulations and Rules, despite several requests, has violated the Organization's regulations and has unfairly prejudiced my employment opportunities at the World Health Organization and in the United Nations system* since international organizations systematically ask individuals who apply for positions to present at least one evaluation report from a previous employer and since I was unable to provide it to the Organizations that requested it;

t. The consequences of the procedural irregularities have caused me moral harm, which deserves compensation.

173. In witness whereof, I respectfully request the Appeals Committee of the Headquarters to recommend to the Director General of: Pay me the salaries and allowances that I would have received if my appointment had been renewed until November 9, 2009, given that my temporary employment contract was implicitly renewed for a further period of twelve months;

a. Pay me the salaries and allowances that I would have received if my appointment had been renewed since November 10th, 2009, until the date on which the administration takes a new decision as to whether or not to renew my contract, since the contractual relations that bound me to WHO continue until a valid decision terminating my appointment has been taken by the Administration;

b. Cancel the decision not to renew my engagement;

c. Reinstate me as an administration officer in the service of the World Health Organization with retroactive effect to November 10th, 2009;

d. Remove from my personal file the unilateral "Evaluation report" prepared by my superior and all defamatory and *falsified documents and send me written confirmation of the list of documents concerned;*

e. *Issue a written apology and ensure its wide dissemination within the World Health Organization for violating my right to be treated fairly, honestly, and honorably;*

f. *Provide me with a certificate in accordance with article 1095 of the Staff Regulations and Status;*

g. *Pay me damages in compensation for the moral harm that my family and I suffered as a result of the malicious attitudes and arbitrary decisions of the Administration.*

Section 5. Method of examination and composition of the Committee

- *Behind closed doors, based solely on written documents.*
- *No objections to the composition of the Committee.*

10-05-2010

Nour-Eddine Benakezouh

Modern Day Slavery

Section 6. LIST OF ANNEXES

1. *Temporary Engagement*
2. *PMDS Form*
3. *Email August 26, 26th 2008, from Mrs. Marie Louise Omog to the Representatives and Administration officers of the Country Offices.*
4. *Email August 29, 2008, from Mr. Andres Nzang stressing the great importance of the GSM awareness and training workshop.*
5. *Email August 29, 2008, from Mrs. Marie Louise Omog to Representatives and Administration officers.*
6. *Email 29 August 2008 de M. Nour-Eddine Benakezouh au Dr Oladapo Walker.*
7. *Email 30 August 2008 from M. Nour-Eddine Benakezouh to Mrs. Marie-Louise Omog.*
8. *Email September 1, 2008, from Mr. Andres Nzang to Representatives and Administration officers.*
9. *Email September 11, 2008, from Dr Fatoumata Binta Diallo to regional bureau.*
10. *Email October 2, 2008, from Dr Fatoumata Binta Diallo to officials of the WHO Representation Office in Mali.*
11. *Email du 6 October 2008 from Dr Fatoumata Binta Diallo to Mr. Nour-Eddine Benakezouh.*
12. *Email October 7, 2008, from Dr Fatoumata Binta Diallo, official of the WHO Representation Office in Mali.*

13. *Email October 8, 2008, from Dr Fatoumata Binta Diallo, officials of the WHO Representation Office in Mali.*

14. *Email October 10, 2008, from Dr Fatoumata Binta Diallo to Mr. Haarman, Administration and Finance Director, with copies to Mr. Durao, Mr. Wadda, and Mr. Benakezouh.*

15. *Email October 10, 2008, from Dr Fatoumata Binta Diallo to Mr. Haarman, Administration and Finance Director, with copies to Mr. Durao and Mr. Wadda.*

16. *Email October 11, 2008, from Mr. Haarman to Dr Fatoumata Binta Diallo et à Mr. Durao with a copy to Mr. Wadda.*

17. *Email 13 October 2008 from Mr. Benakezouh à Mr. Haarman et Dr Diallo avec copies à Mr. Durao et Mr. Wadda.*

18. *Email dated October 14 from Dr Diallo to Mr. Haarman and Mr. Durao with copies to Mr. Wadda and Mr. Benakezouh.*

19. *Evaluation report of Dr Diallo.*

20. *Email October 15, 2008, from Mr. Benakezouh to Dr. Diallo, Mr. Haarman, and Mr. Durao with a copy to Mr. Wadda.*

21. *Email October 22, 2008, from Mr. Benakezouh à Mr. Haarman and Mr. Durao with copies to Dr Diallo and Mr. Wadda.*

22. *Email October 27, 2008, from Mt. Haarman to Dr Diallo with a copy to Mr. Benakezouh.*

23. *Memorandum of November 5, 2008. Object: End of your commitment.*

24. *Memorandum du 05 November 2008. Object: End of engagement formalities.*

25. *Email 05 November 2008 from Mr. Benakezouh à Mr. Durao.*

26. *Email November 7, 2008, from Mr. Charlemagne Pissara, compliance officer.*

27. *Email December 13, 2008, from Mr. Benakezouh to Mr. Durao with copies to Mr. Haarman, Dr Sambo, and Dr. Diallo.*

28. *Email December 13, 2008, from Dr Sambo à Mr. Durao and Mr. Benakezouh with a copy to Mr. Haarman.*

29. *Email December 15, 2008, from Mr. Durao to Mr. Benakezouh and Email December 15, 2008, from Mr. Benakezouh to Mr. Durao.*

30. *Email 18 January 2009 from Mr. Benakezouh to M. Durao, M. Haarman et au Dr Sambo.*

31. *Email du 26 January 2009 de Mr. Benakezouh à Mr. Durao, Mr. Haarman and Dr Sambo.*

32. *Emails on January 27 from Mr. Durao to Mr. Benakezouh and 29 Janvier, 2009, from Mr. Tagnon to Mr. Benakezouh.*

33. *Email 13 September 2009 from Mr. Benakezouh to M. Durao.*

34. *Article 1095 of Staff Regulations and Staff Rules.*

35. *Email 18 September 2009 from Mr. Wadda to Mr. Benakezouh.*

36. *Certificate dated September 16, 2009, and signed by Mr. Alvaro Durao.*

37. *Email dated September 24, 2009, from Mr. Benakezouh to Mr. Durao.*

38. *Emails of October 05, 14, 27, and November 6, 2009, from Mr. Benakezouh.*

39. *Email from UNRWA to Mr. Benakezouh.*

40. *Email From the United Nations to Mr. Benakezouh.*

41. *Email from UNOWA to Mr. Benakezouh.*

42. *Email From WHO Geneva to Mr. Benakezouh.*

43. *Email From UNOPS to Mr. Benakezouh.*

44. *Email From the World Bank to Mr. Benakezouh.*

45. *Email 28 September 2009 from Mrs. Mouzinga to Mr. Benakezouh.*

46. *Email 28 September 2009 from Mr. Benakezouh to Mrs. Mandzoungou (RAC).*

47. *Email 29 September 2009 from Mrs. Mandzoungou (RAC) to Mr. Benakezouh.*

48. *Request for review of the decision addressed to Mr. Regional Director.*

49. *Email 17 November 2009 from Mr. Benakezouh to Mr. Durao.*

50. *Email 23 November 2009 from Mr. Benakezouh to Mrs. Mandzoungou (RAC).*

51. *Email 13 December 2009 from Mr. Benakezouh to Mrs. Mandzoungou (RAC).*

52. *Email 18 January 2010 from Mrs. Mandzoungou (RAC) to Mr. Benakezouh.*

53. *Email 25 January 2009 from Mr. Benakezouh to Mrs. Mandzoungou (RAC).*

54. *Email 28 January 2010 from Mrs. Mandzoungou (RAC) à Mr. Benakezouh.*

55. *Email 05 February 2010 from Mrs. Mandzoungou (RAC) to Mr. Benakezouh.*

56. *Letter February 4, 2010, from M. Pule, president of RAC.*

57. *AFRO-MEMORANDUM of Mr. Durao February 2, 2010.*

58. *Email 11 February 2010 from Mr. Benakezouh to Mrs. Mandzoungou (RAC).*

59. *Response from Mr. Benakezouh on February 11, 2010.*

60. *Email 09 April 2010 from Mr. Éric Tagnon to Mr. Benakezouh.*

61. *Letter from the Regional Director on April 9, 2010, notifying his final decision.*

62. *Report of the Regional Appeal Committee*

The WHO Directorate General responded, through Mr. Farice Quinio, Human Resources Specialist, to my Appeal against the Regional Director's decision on June 30th, 2010.

Mr. Quinio repeated the Regional Director song by asking the Committee to reject the Applicant's requests for the following reasons:

a) The decision of the Regional Director of April 9th, 2010, to declare the Applicant's Appeal inadmissible because his declaration indicating his intention to appeal was not served within the statutory time limits was well founded on the basis of the provisions of Article 1230.8 of the Staff Regulations.

b) In any event, even if the Applicant's Appeal were admissible, the administration has demonstrated that by giving a one-month notice period, the Organization complied with its obligations, as contained in the Staff Regulations and Rules.

c) Finally, the non-extension of the Applicant's temporary appointment is not linked to considerations of the Applicant's performance evaluation but is explained by the Regional Director's decision to reassign a staff member with a fixed-term appointment.

The WHO general management was no different from the regional management in handling the case. It did everything it could to avoid answering the questions it had to answer if it wanted to maintain a minimum of credibility.

The WHO general management had a choice to make, and it opted for the alternative that was least damaging to WHO in terms of reputation. If the management had questioned Dr. Sambo's decision, it would have been forced to get to the bottom of things to understand the reason for all the abuses of power.

The WHO General Management was not, at all, interested in doing this exercise because they knew very well that all their paths in this exercise led to Luanda. The General Management did not want to hear about Luanda because Luanda, in our case, was the hometown of the little Angolan girl. As a result, Luanda became, by the force of Dr. Diallo, synonymous with Modern-Day Slavery and rape of minors. The General Management of the WHO did not want to hear about these terms because, even though they were happening in the organization, they were banned from the Organization's dictionary.

Unable to make the right but difficult choice, the general management found itself doing gymnastics to make the articles of the staff regulations and the decisions of the United Nations Tribunal say what they had never said.

I can easily understand that as a human resources specialist, Mr. Farice Quinio is not able to interpret the decisions of the United Nations Tribunals, which he cites without taking the trouble to give the judgment numbers, but not understanding the articles of the Staff Regulations and Staff Rules, which he cites at random, is something that is beyond me.

I will simply share what I told the Appeals Committee of the Headquarters.

HEADQUARTERS APPEAL COMMITTEE
CASE No 755 – M. Nour-Eddine Benakezouh (AFRO)

APPLICANT'S RESPONSE

In accordance with the provisions of Article 26 of the Internal Regulations of the Headquarters Appeals Committee (CAS), I submit a written reply to the official response of the administration in strict compliance with the deadline of ten working days as stipulated in the article mentioned above.

I am using the format used by the Administration in its response to my brief in order to simplify things.

In sections 3, 4, and 5, I reply to all the Administration's responses, keeping the same paragraph numbers to facilitate comparison of the arguments.

1. **SUMMARY OF THE CALL**

   1.1. As compensation, I respectfully request the Appeals Committee of the Headquarters to recommend to the Director General to:

      1.1.1. Pay me the salaries and allowances that I would have received if my appointment had been renewed until November 9, 2009, given that my temporary employment contract was implicitly renewed for a further period of twelve months;

      1.1.2. Pay me the salaries and allowances that I would have received if my appointment had been renewed since November 10, 2009, until the date on which the Administration takes a new decision as to whether or *not to renew my contract since the contractual relations that bound me to WHO continue until a valid decision terminating my appointment has been taken by the Administration;*

1.1.3. *Cancel the decision not to renew my engagement;*

1.1.4. *Reinstate me as an administration officer in the service of the World Health Organization with retroactive effect to November 10, 2009;*

1.1.5. *Remove from my personal file the unilateral "evaluation report" prepared by my superior and all defamatory and falsified documents and send me written confirmation of the list of documents concerned;*

1.1.6. *Issue a written apology and ensure its wide dissemination within the World Health Organization for violating my right to be treated fairly, honestly, and honorably;*

1.1.7. *Provide me with a certificate in accordance with article 1095 of the Staff Regulations and Status;*

1.1.8. *Pay me damages in compensation for the moral harm that my family and I suffered as a result of the malicious attitudes and arbitrary decisions of the Administration.*

2. APPLICANT'S SERVICE STATUS

2.1. *I joined the WHO Representation Office in Mali on November 9, 2007, as an administration officer, under a temporary appointment for a period of one year, which was to end on November 9, 2008.*

2.2. *In accordance with my contract, I was to receive notice of non-extension no later than October 10, 2008. However, it was only on November 5, 2008, that I received the notice dated the same day.*

2.3. *Since I did not receive notice within the prescribed period, my appointment was implicitly renewed for another year.*

2.4. *In the absence of a valid decision terminating my appointment, the contractual relations between me and WHO continue.*

3. ADMISSIBILITY

3.1. *It is very important at this level of the argument to note that Article 1230.8.3 of the Staff Regulations states that the period of 60 calendar days following receipt of the notification applies to the declaration of intention to appeal and not to the complete declaration.*

3.2. *Staff Rule 1230.8.1 states: "A staff member may appeal to a committee only when all existing administrative remedies have been exhausted and the action complained of has become final. An action is considered final when it has been taken by a duly authorized official and the staff member has been notified in writing."*

3.3. *Staff Rule 1230.8.3 clearly states: "A staff member who wishes to appeal a final action shall, within 60 calendar days of receipt of the notification, submit in writing to the appropriate committee a statement indicating his or her intention to appeal, specifying the action being appealed and the subsection(s) of Staff Rule 1230.1 that he or she* is invoking for this purpose." On November 5, 2008, I received notification that my temporary appointment would not be renewed. I was a staff member on November 5, 2008. Staff Rule 1230.8.3 gave me 60 calendar days to submit a written statement of intent to appeal. I, therefore, had until January 5, 2009, to make my statement of intent to appeal.

3.4. In addition to Staff Rule 1230.8.3, the WHO Administration, in its response of February 2, 2010, to my appeal brief to the Regional Appeals Board, citing the same rule, states that I had 60 days to submit my statement of intent to appeal. Today, the Administration argues that I should have submitted my statement of intent 30 days after receipt of the final decision, not 60 days after receipt of the final decision.

3.5. The Administration's assertion that: "It was only on January 25, 2010, more than 14 months after receiving notification of the decision not to extend his temporary appointment, that the applicant filed his declaration indicating his intention to appeal" is erroneous. It is further proof of the Administration's bad faith, which is conflating the declaration of intention to appeal with the full declaration of the Appeal.

This conflating is intentionally done by the Administration to support a flawed argument that needs this conflating to be supported. My declaration of intention to appeal on December 13, 2008, in full compliance with Article 1230.8.3 of the Staff Regulations.

3.6. The decision of the Regional Director to dismiss my Appeal as inadmissible cannot be right because it is *based on the recommendation of the WHO Regional Appeals Board, which made serious errors of fact and law in its report to the WHO Regional Director. These errors have all been highlighted in paragraphs 78 to 86 of my submission to the Headquarters Appeals Board to enable them to assess the situation at its true value.*

3.7. *In addition to knowing the reasons for the decision not to renew my appointment in order to adequately prepare my Appeal, I also wanted to ensure that all administrative remedies had been exhausted and to have the contact details of the Regional Appeals Committee. To this end, I tried to contact Mr. Alvaro Durao, Regional Personnel Administration officer, by telephone, on November 5, 2008, the day I received the notification not to extend my temporary appointment.*

3.8. *I left two messages in Mr. Durao's voicemail in which I explained that I wanted to know the reasons for the decision in order to adequately prepare my Appeal. I also asked him to send me a copy of the Internal Regulations of the Regional Appeals Committee as well as the contact details of the latter's secretariat.*

3.9. *Having not heard from Mr. Durao throughout the day, I sent him an email at the end of the day. Having received no reply to my email either, I tried to obtain advice from Mr. Charlemagne Pissara, compliance officer, who, in his email of November 7, 2008, had suggested that I try to contact Mr. Durao again.*

3.10. *The regulatory provisions applicable to the WHO internal appeals system (article 1230.8.1 of the Staff Regulations) recognize that referral to the Appeals*

Committee is subject to the condition that all existing "administrative appeals" have been exhausted beforehand. I was therefore obliged to contact the Administration first to ensure that the existing "administrative appeals" have been exhausted.

3.11. *In view of the refusal of the Regional Personnel Officer to respond to my correspondence, I sent another email to Mr. Durao on December 13, 2008 in wish I copied Mr. Sander Edward Haarman, Regional Director of Administration and Finance; Dr. Luis Gomes Sambo, Regional Director, Dr Margaret Chan, Director-General of WHO; and Dr. Fatoumata Binta Diallo, WHO Representative in Mali. My email of December 13, 2008, constitutes my declaration of intention to appeal, and this declaration was made 39 days after receipt of the decision not to renew my appointment, in accordance with the provision of Staff Rule 1230.8.3. I had neither the internal regulations nor the contact details of the Regional Appeals Committee, and Mr. Durao refused to send them to me and to respond to my requests for explanations even though he had clearly indicated to me in his November 5, 2008 memorandum, that "We remain at your disposal for any information you may need." The Representative had asked me to leave the work offices the same day. It took the intervention of certain officials for her to let me prepare my handover to the Administrative Assistant. Knowing the actions of the Representative, I wanted to take stock of the situation before leaving. From November 12, 2008, the Representative had forbidden me access to my office even though my contract ended on December 5, 2008, and I had been paid until that day. I found myself cut off from the rest of the world overnight, without a computer, without internet, etc.*

3.12. *I have clearly identified the decision being challenged, the decision to terminate my employment contract with the WHO, and I have listed the grounds invoked for the evaluation. Indeed, in the email of December 13, 2008, I wrote the following: "I find it unfortunate and regrettable that you did not take the time to contact me to clarify the things contained in your memos informing me of your decision to terminate my employment contract with the WHO. A decision that was motivated by the unilateral "evaluation" submitted to you by the WHO representative in Mali under conditions that you know as well as I do. An evaluation that is an evaluation in name only since it is much more a demonization of me than anything else.*

3.13. *According to case law, an organization must interpret an agent's statements according to the rules of good faith; required to avoid unnecessary harm to the agent, it can also be called upon to guide him in his steps and to dispel any error. The Administration did none of this. On the contrary, it chose to ignore my two messages left in Mr. Durao's voicemail on November 5, 2008, and the email sent the same day to the same person. It is astonishing to see the Administration today arguing that I had not contacted the Regional Appeals Committee in time when the Regional Personnel Administrator refused to provide me with a copy of the RAC's internal regulations and the contact details of the letter's secretariat in order to formulate my appeal adequately. The Administration failed in its duty of care incumbent on an international organization towards its officials, by refusing to respond to my correspondence. It is this failure that is the source of these questions.*

The ILO Administrative Tribunal had to rule on the argument of the formalization of the appeal, dear to the Administration. In its judgment, no. 1167, where the WHO was the defendant organization, the ILO Administrative Tribunal stated, "**Secondly, article 1230.8.3, on which the contested decision is based, does not require that the file submitted within the appeal period be complete. On the contrary, for the appeal to be admissible, it is necessary and sufficient that the contested decision be clearly identified and that the grounds invoked be listed.**"

3.14. *It is true that paragraph 1230.8.3 of Article 1230 of the Staff Regulations stipulates that my declaration of intent should be addressed to the relevant committee, namely the Regional Appeals Board. But it is also true, according to case law, that submitting an appeal to an incompetent body of an organization is sufficient to respect a deadline, the incompetent body being required to forward the appeal in question to the competent body.*

In its judgment, no. 2017, the ILO Administrative Tribunal considered in particular that, "**Submitting an act to an incompetent body of an organization is sufficient to ensure compliance with a deadline, the incompetent body being required to forward the act in question to the competent body.**"

Surprisingly, the administration initially refused to provide me with a copy of the Internal Regulations and the contact details of the Regional Appeals Board, only to argue later that I had not referred the matter to the RAC in time.

3.15. *The administration's persistence in submitting erroneous information regarding the date of my declaration of intention to appeal the decision, for the second time in its response (see 3.5), proves, if need be, that the Administration has difficulty in providing arguments based on the real facts. The detailed chronology of events contained in section II of my appeal brief submitted to the CAS clearly illustrates the dates of all the events, despite the Administration's persistence in saying that it was only on January 25, 2010, that the applicant filed his declaration of intention to appeal.*

3.16. *Article 1230.8.1 of the Staff Regulations refers to existing administrative remedies without naming them or specifying their nature. I was therefore forced to contact the Administration first to ensure that all existing administrative remedies to which Article 1230.8.1 of the Staff Regulations could refer had been exhausted and that the measure that is the subject of the complaint had become final in order to properly appeal the decision. The refusal of the Regional Personnel Administrator to respond to my requests (two telephone messages and an email) caused things to take a different turn and not my carelessness or passivity. I even contacted the compliance officer to find out what to do in the face of the Regional Personnel Administrator's administration's refusal to respond to my communications. His response was simple, "Continue to try to contact the Regional Personnel Administrator."*

3.17. *I did not actually take any steps that could be considered an "appeal" during the period mentioned by the Administration for the simple reason that I was not at the stage of doing so.*

My first concern upon receiving notification of the non-renewal of my temporary appointment was to know the reasons. I could not take any steps in the sense that I did not know the reasons for the decision, which should logically dictate the direction of the steps I should take.

3.18. *My email of November 5, 2008, was not a formal appeal.*

3.19. *The interpretation that the Administration makes of the message from the Regional Director of December 13, 2008, to the Regional Personnel Administration and of the message that the Regional Personnel Administrator sent to me on December 15, 2008, following the message from the Regional Director, is very different from the interpretation that I make of it and that any person acting in good faith can make of it.*

The Regional Director made a point of sending a message to the Regional Personnel Administrator within minutes of sending my email while he was outside the continent where he was working, demonstrating the seriousness with which the latter took my correspondence, which has unfortunately never been the case for the Regional Personnel Officer (RPO).

In his email, the Director clearly told the Regional Personnel Administrator: "RPO, I think we should hear the petitioner." As for the email of December 15, 2010, from the Regional Personnel Officer, it was not just a request for telephone contacts, as the Administration claims, which is trying by all means to reduce the importance of this document.

The Regional Personnel Officer, after 45 days of radio silence, replied to my email and asked for my telephone number in order to hear me as the Director General suggested and not to wish me the best wishes (Christmas and New Year). It is very important to note that the Regional Director insisted on copying me in the email he sent to the Regional Personnel Officer.

3.20. *What is incorrect is repeating a false statement several times in the hope of having it accepted by force of circumstance. Once again, my declaration of intention to appeal the decision not to extend my temporary appointment was not made on January 25, 2010, but rather on December 13, 2008.*

3.21. *Following my email of December 13, 2008, in which I explicitly linked the decision not to extend my appointment to the unilateral evaluation prepared by my superior by stating the following, "I find it unfortunate and regrettable that you did not take the time to contact me to clarify the things contained in your memos informing me of your decision to terminate my employment contract with the WHO. A decision that was motivated by the unilateral "evaluation" submitted to you by the WHO representative in Mali under conditions that you know as well as I do. An evaluation that is an evaluation in name only since it is much more a demonization of me than anything else.*

To achieve her goals, the WHO representative in Mali resorted to lies, half-truths, and falsification of documents that she attached as annexes to her "evaluation" and that she only made available to me after the intervention of Mr. Sander E. Haarman asking her to give me a copy of these documents as soon as possible in accordance with the regulations and practices in this type of situation," the Regional Director felt the need to intervene by telling the Regional Personnel Administrator that he thought I should be heard.

The latter, after 45 days of disregard, took the trouble to send me an email apologizing for his silence and asking me to give him my telephone number in Montreal. Any person of good faith will come to the conclusion that the email sent to me by the Regional Personnel Officer is linked to the email of December 13, 2008, from the Regional Director in which he suggested that he hear me.

3.22. *The Organization had not responded to my letter of October 11, 2009, for reasons other than those given in the Administration's response. Indeed, in this 53-page letter with 97 annexes, I responded to the accusations made against me by the WHO Representative in Mali in her unilateral "evaluation." I also informed the Regional Director of the threats to the financial and other interests of the WHO Representation in Mali.*

I tried with all conscience, perhaps naively, to protect the interests of WHO in Mali. This did not please the WHO

Representative in Mali, who resorted to lies, half-truths, and falsification of documents to terminate my temporary appointment.

I say naively because the Administration was aware of the actions of the Representative in Angola, where she was the WHO Representative before her assignment to Mali. During the GSM awareness workshop, which took place in Gaborone, Botswana, from 18 to September 22, 2008, I asked to meet Mr. Haarman, DAF, to tell him about my concerns about the actions of the Representative.

I was relieved to learn through Mr. Haarman that the WHO Administrator in Angola had informed him of the same actions of the Representative when she was in Angola. Mr. Haarman had advised me to document all my concerns.

All this to say that the administration's explanations concerning the reasons why the Regional Director had not responded to my letter are not convincing, especially since the Administration did not consider it useful to give the reasons why the Regional Personnel Officer had not responded to my other correspondence. The answer is simple and painful: this is an abuse of power.

3.23. The statement of intent to appeal was submitted to the Regional Personnel Officer on December 13, 2008, and not on January 25, 2010, as the Administration continues to assert. The decision of the Regional Director to dismiss my appeal as inadmissible cannot be fair since it is based on the recommendation of the WHO Regional Appeals Board, which made serious errors of fact and law in its report to the WHO Regional Director. These errors were all highlighted in paragraphs 78 to 86 of my submission to the Headquarters Appeals Board to enable them to assess the situation at its true value.

3.24. Not as convinced of the inadmissibility of my appeal as it has publicly suggested, the Administration is resorting to the confusion between the declaration of intention to appeal, referred to in Article 1230.8.3 of the Staff Rules, and the complete declaration to give credibility to its argument.

The ILO Administrative Tribunal ruled specifically on this article in its judgment number 1167, in which it stated, **"Secondly, Article 1230.8.3, on which the decision appealed is based, does not require that the file submitted within the appeal period be complete. On the contrary, for the appeal to be admissible, it is necessary and sufficient that the decision appealed be clearly identified and that the grounds invoked be listed."**

The administration has also resorted to repeating false assertions in the hope of making them more plausible. The claim that I did not submit my notice of intention to appeal until January 25, 2010, is a perfect example of this.

4. **REPLY TO THE ADMINISTRATION'S RESPONSE**

<u>The question does not arise in terms of the reasonableness of the notice periods but rather in terms of compliance with the time limit prescribed for notification of non-renewal of an engagement.</u>

4.1. Judgment number 2531 of the ILO Administrative Tribunal, cited by the Administration, concerns an organization, the WTO, whose Staff Rules do not contain any provision requiring notice in the event of non-renewal of a contract of a staff member engaged for a short period. In this case, the problem may arise in terms of the reasonableness of the deadlines. The question, in the case before us, arises in terms of compliance with the provisions of the Staff Rules since paragraph 1 of Article 1040 of the WHO Staff Rules, under which the Administration decided not to offer me an extension of my temporary appointment, clearly states: "Where it has been decided not to offer an extension to a staff member engaged on a temporary basis, the latter shall be notified of this fact normally not later than one month before the expiry date of the appointment." Judgment number 2531 of the ILO Administrative Tribunal is, therefore, not relevant.

4.2. Judgments 2750 and 2104 are not relevant to the case before us for the same reasons developed above for judgment number 2531. Indeed, the issue before us is a question of compliance with the time limit prescribed in the Staff Regulations and not of the need for reasonable time limits. Judgment number 1374 of the Administrative Tribunal of the ILO stated, "The need for a decision of non-renewal, even in the case of temporary appointment, arises upon completion of the agreed period of service. The decision of the Administration not to renew the appointment must be notified within the prescribed time limit. In the absence of notice within the time limit, the contract is implicitly renewed for a new period."

4.3. I joined the WHO Representative Office in Mali on November 9, 2007 under a one-year temporary appointment that was due to end on November 9, 2008. In accordance with my contract and Staff Rule 1040.1, I was to receive notice of non-extension by October 10, 2008, at the latest. However, it was not until November 5, 2008, that I received the notice dated the same day. Since I did not receive notice within the prescribed period, my appointment was implicitly renewed for another year. In its judgment 1040, the ILO Administrative Tribunal stated that, "The complainant Complainant's three-month appointment was due to end on October 9, 1987. In accordance with his contract, he was to receive fifteen days before that date, that is to say, on September 24, 1987, his notice of non-extension. However, it was not until September 28, 1987, that he received the notice. In these circumstances, the Tribunal considers that his appointment was extended until January 9, 1988. The extension of his contract by five days until October 14, 1987, in order to complete the period of notice provided for, was ineffective because the notice was late."

4.4. Once again, the issue is not one of the needs for reasonable notice but rather of compliance with the Staff Regulations of the Organization. I submitted my declaration of intention to appeal the decision not to renew my temporary appointment on December 13, 2008, and not on January 25, 2010, as the administration likes to repeat in order to confuse the declaration of intention to appeal with the full declaration.

4.5. *The administration did not go beyond Article 1040.1 of the Staff Regulations. The article in question includes five (5) paragraphs. The Administration only cites, for reasons that I really do not understand, the first paragraph. My astonishment is mainly due to the fact that the ILO Administrative Tribunal had to rule on this argument of the WHO (Judgment number 469) because of its ambiguity.*

4.6. *My position on the notice period is based on judgment number 469 of the ILO Administrative Tribunal. If the WHO had any problem with the validity of the Tribunal's decision, it should have challenged the decision since it was the defendant's Organization in the judgment in question. In addition, the WHO Regulations do not mention the consequences of non-compliance with Article 1040, paragraph 1 of the Staff Rules, which states, "The need for a decision of non-renewal, even in the case of temporary appointment, arises upon completion of the agreed period of service. The decision of the Administration not to renew the appointment must be notified within the prescribed period. In the absence of notice within the period, the contract is implicitly renewed for a new period."*

4.7. *The ILO Administrative Tribunal, in its judgment number 469, had to rule on the ambiguity of WHO Staff Rule 1040.1. The latter stated that: "The text of Staff Rule 1040 is not absolutely clear and unambiguous, since there may be a conflict between the provision that the appointment terminates automatically and the need for a decision not to renew.*

However, according to the Tribunal's consistent interpretation, this text, as well as similar provisions in other organizations, must be considered as requiring a decision by the Director-General not to renew the appointment (a decision over which the Tribunal has only limited power of review) and its notification to the staff member before the prescribed date.

To interpret it to mean that the appointment automatically terminates on the date of its expiry, whether or not there has been notice, would violate this article by making the provision relating to notice superfluous and would, moreover, be unreasonable and unfair: it would mean that a staff member who, like the applicant, has been in the service of the Organization for seven years could be dismissed without notice at the end of the period. What, then, is the effect of the absence of notice?

In the eyes of the Tribunal, there can be only one, namely that the contract is implicitly renewed for a new period."
I, therefore, do not understand the Administration's recourse to Judgment 2162, which is not as relevant as Judgment number 469 since the latter concerns WHO and specifically Article 1040.1. Article under which my appointment was not extended.

4.8. *I do not believe that the Organization has complied with its obligations since its notice was late. In addition to judgment number 469, in which WHO was a defendant, judgment number 1374 of the ILO Administrative Tribunal stated,* **"The need for a decision of non-renewal, even in the case of temporary appointment,** *arises upon completion of the agreed period of service. The decision of the Administration not to renew the appointment must be notified within the prescribed period. In the absence of notice within the period, the contract is implicitly renewed for a new period."*

<u>**A temporary engagement, just like a fixed-term contract, gives rights and imposes obligations on the parties.**</u>

4.9. *I clearly stated in my brief that I had a temporary appointment that gave me rights that I was trying to assert. What is especially important to emphasize is the fact that my contract, contrary to what the Administration claims, is not short-term. Short-term contracts are contracts of less than 11 months. The WHO makes a very clear distinction between contracts of less than and more than 11 months in its regulations. This is not the first time that the Administration has made this amalgam. The Regional Appeals Committee was misled. It, therefore, wrongly stated in its report that I had an 11-month contract.*

4.10. *Far be it from me to lump things together. I am a civil servant who is convinced that I have been the victim of injustice, and I am trying to defend myself as best I can. Once again, the Administration must specify its assertions and not resort to generalities. It is rather the Administration that is resorting to lumping things together to give credibility to its arguments. Indeed, the Administration prefers to talk about the distinctions between UNESCO short-term contracts and fixed-term contracts rather than the distinctions that WHO makes between these contracts because it knows that the provisions of the Staff Regulations on contracts do not support the arguments put forward by the Administration.*

4.11. *Judgment No. 1560 of the ILO Administrative Tribunal doesn't distinguish between short-term contracts and fixed-term contracts. It does so in a manner specific to UNESCO, which is the Organization responding to that judgment. The Tribunal specified that this is the distinction made by the UNESCO Staff Regulations and Rules. As each Organization has its own Staff Regulations, it would have been preferable for the Administration to explain to us the distinction made by the WHO Staff Regulations between the different contracts because the provisions of the WHO Staff Regulations, in terms of contracts, are completely different from those of the UNESCO Staff Regulations. If there is any case law in Judgment No. 1560 of the Tribunal, it is that of the importance of respecting the Organization's Staff Regulations.*

4.12. *Judgment No. 2198 of the ILO Administrative Tribunal does not at any time refer to the notion of motivation for a decision not to renew a contract for the simple reason that it did not have to rule on this subject. What it said concerning the discretionary power of the executive is valid for both temporary and fixed-term appointments. In fact, the United Nations Administrative Tribunal has repeatedly stated that the Administration enjoys discretionary power in matters of renewal or non-renewal of an appointment and that an appointment, if not renewed, ends with the passage of time as provided for in the appointment itself. (Judgments No. 440 and No. 1003). However, the established jurisprudence of the United Nations*

Administrative Tribunal is that the exercise of this discretionary power must not be tainted by caprice, bias, falsehoods, or serious breach of due process. This discretionary power must be exercised without the intervention of any irregular motivation so as to avoid an abuse of power (Judgments 50, 109, 142, 319 and 345).

4.13. *The administration did not act in accordance with the jurisprudence because its decision not to renew my temporary appointment was tainted by serious breaches of due process guarantees that led to a serious abuse of authority. In its judgment number 1052, the United Nations Administrative Tribunal stated that the lack of motivation for the decision not to renew can also be considered a serious procedural flaw. "The fact that no reason was given, which can be considered contrary to a general principle of the international civil service requiring the motivation of decisions - even discretionary ones - concerning the career of international civil servants. This situation opens the door wide to the total arbitrariness." The Administration recognizes my right to appeal the decision not to renew my temporary appointment while arguing that the Director General has the discretionary power to renew or not my temporary appointment. These two assertions are contradictory. If the decision not to renew my appointment is subject to appeal, it must be justified so that the person concerned can assert their rights.*

4.14. *Consistent case law shows that the service contract has the effect of creating a public law employment relationship, inserted in a statutory and administrative context from which requirements or consequences may arise that go beyond the framework of the contractual relationship itself. Thus, reinstatement may be considered, even in the case of a limited-term contract, in exceptional situations, when an organization systematically uses such contracts to deal with permanent administrative tasks, when a contractual relationship has been vitiated by unacceptable administrative practices, or when the untimely non-renewal of a contract has the effect of depriving an employee of his or her pension rights.*

4.15. *I request that due process be afforded and that due process guarantees be respected.*

4.16. *I do not see the relevance of judgment number 2850 to the case before us. In its judgment number 1052, the United Nations Administrative Tribunal stated that the absence of reasons for the decision of non-renewal can also be considered a serious procedural defect. "The fact that no reasons were given, which can be considered contrary to a general principle of the international civil service requiring the motivation of decisions - even discretionary ones - concerning the career of international civil servants. This situation opens the door wide to the most total arbitrariness.*

4.17. *I do not see the relevance of judgment number 2308 to the case before us.*

4.18. *The established jurisprudence of the United Nations Administrative Tribunal is that the exercise of the discretionary power of the Director-General must not be tainted by caprice, bias, falsehood, or serious breach of due process. This discretionary power must be exercised without the intervention of any improper motivation so as to avoid an abuse of power. The United Nations Administrative Tribunal stated in its Judgment 885 that the exercise by the Administration of its discretionary power not to renew a contract must not be vitiated by any form of abuse of power and that in the presence of special circumstances, such as in the case of misuse by the Administration of its discretionary power in refusing to renew a contract, the United Nations Administrative Tribunal held, in the same judgment, that an exception could be made to the rule of discretionary power.*

4.19. *In accepting the offer of a temporary appointment on October 31th, 2007, I was convinced that by working for a specialized agency of the U N, the guarantees of due process would be respected and that there were safeguards to prevent any abuse of power. I am still convinced of this and it is in this context that I try to assert my rights.*

Facts speak louder than words. The non-renewal of my contract is closely linked to the unilateral "evaluation report" of my superior.

4.20. *Fortunately, facts speak louder than words. While it is true that at no time was my performance cited in support of the Organization's non-extension of my temporary appointment, the fact remains that the facts preceding the contested decision clearly show the link between the non-renewal of my appointment and the unilateral "Evaluation Report" prepared by my superior. These facts were set out in my appeal brief. In what follows, I will simply highlight two events that are important for understanding the real reasons for the non-renewal of my contract.*

4.21. On Friday, October 10th, 2008, at 10:02, my superior sent an email (Annex A 14) to Mr. Haarman, Director of Administration and Finance, with copies to Mr. Durao, Regional Personnel Administrator, to Mr. Wadda and to myself, telling him that I was unable to send him my PMDS and that she would send him her evaluation unilaterally. On the same day, October 10th, 2008, at 15:20, my superior sent another email (A 15) to Mr. Haarman with copies to Mr. Durao and Mr. Wadda asking them to, "Note that the start date of Mr. Nour's contract is November 9th, 2007 instead of November 14th." My superior did not send me a copy of this email. The two emails suggest that on that day, there was a discussion about my engagement between my superior and the regional management. My Representative sent him a second one to confirm or rectify an error concerning the start of my contract. These facts establish the link, if need be, between my evaluation and the non-renewal of my contract.

4.22. Between September 18th and September 22nd, 2008, the GSM awareness and training workshop was held in Gaborone, Botswana. The implementation of the CSM was going to completely change the way WHO Country Offices operated. Hence the great importance of this workshop to which, among others, all the Representatives and Administrators of the Country Offices were invited. My superior spent 11 days doing everything to prevent me from participating in this workshop. Finally, and on the instructions of the Regional Director, I participated in this workshop. Why let me attend a workshop that was taking place three weeks before the date on which the Organization was to notify me of the decision to renew or *not my appointment and whose work was preparing the Representatives and Administrators for the implementation of the GSM that would take place after the end of my contract if it had been decided not to renew my contract. The answer is simple: At that date, it was a question of renewing my appointment.*

4.23. *This argument is far from convincing. If that were the case, the administration could have renewed my contract until January 2009, the date on which the new administrator took office. This would have allowed me to hand over the contract and ensure a smooth transition. This would have allowed me to assist the WHO Representation Office in Mali during the Global Ministerial Forum on Research for Health (17 to November 19, 2008), for which I was a member of the organizing committee. What happened is completely the opposite of that. The administration asked me to hand over WHO property on the same day that the decision was handed to me (November 5th, 2008), by Dr. Diallo who asked me to leave the workplace on November 7th, 2008, although I continued to be paid until December 5th, 2008. I do not believe, in light of that, that the conduct of the administration is due to the decision to transfer a member of Staff hired for a fixed period.*

4.24. *If this was the case, why did the reassigned staff member not attend the GSM awareness and training workshop in Gaborone, Botswana?*

4.25. *The Administration is free to answer or not to answer the questions. The members of the Appeals Committee of the Headquarters must assess things at their true value because the refusal to answer is an answer in itself.*

4.26. I submitted my statement of intent to appeal in accordance with the requirements of WHO Staff Rule 1230.1.

4.27. This is apparently not my conclusion.

5. CONCLUSION

5.1. The April 9th, 2010 decision of the WHO Regional Director, cannot be well founded because it is based on the report of the Regional Appeals Committee. A report which is riddled with serious errors of fact and law. Errors that I took care to list in paragraphs 77 to 86 of my appeal brief submitted to the CAS. The Regional Appeals Committee, in fact, confirmed the inadmissibility of the appeal on the basis, among other things, of Article 540.1.3 of the Staff Regulations and the Staff Regulations. The CAR went so far as to state that Article 540.1.3 related to the "end of engagements," whereas it concerns the "end of the probationary period."

5.2. The administration knows full well that my appeal is admissible. It is nevertheless attacking its admissibility because it knows full well that there were serious breaches of due process guarantees. These violations of the Organization's rules and procedures meant that the decision not to renew my temporary appointment was vitiated by a form of abuse of power. By attacking the admissibility of my appeal, the administration wants to ignore all the violations of the rights guaranteed by the Organization's regulations.

5.3. Convinced that its argument that my declaration of intent was made on January 25th, 2010, is not convincing, since I submitted my declaration of intent on December 13th, 2008, the Administration innovates by asserting that I was not a member of staff on December 13th, 2008. Therefore, my appeal is not admissible because it was made after December 5th, 2008, although Article 1230.8.3 of the Staff

Regulations gives me 60 calendar days to submit my declaration of intent to appeal.

It is important, at this level, to note that the administration's position on this specific point has changed over time. In its response of February 2nd, 2010, to the Regional Appeals Committee, the administration maintains that I had 60 calendar days from the time of receipt of notification of the decision not to extend my appointment to declare my intention to appeal.

After arguing, with case law in support, that my intention to appeal declaration was submitted on January 13th, 2008, in strict compliance with the Staff Regulations, the administration came back with a new argument. According to the administration, I had 30 calendar days and not 60 days to appeal.

This new argument would have been more convincing if the administration had boosted it with case law or legal texts.

5.4. *The administration, in its response to my memorandum, categorically refuses to discuss all the violations of the organization's regulations that led to the decision not to renew my appointment. The administration's reasoning is simplistic, to say the least. Since the decision not to renew my appointment falls within the discretionary power of the Director-General, all violations of my right to due process, all violations of established and current procedures, and all abuses of power are permitted. This is in complete contradiction with the consistent case law of the Administrative Tribunal.*

5.5. *The administration has not ruled on my request to remove from my personal file the unilateral "evaluation report" prepared by my superior and all the defamatory and falsified documents since the administration does not contest these allegations.*

5.6. The CAS has also not commented on the refusal of the RPO to provide me with a certificate in accordance with Article 1095 of the Staff Regulations.

5.7. I am not the only one who suffers harm when the administration does not follow its own rules as it should. The entire administrative process is, in fact, undermined when my rights to due process are seriously affected. Scrupulous and impeccable compliance with the procedure established by the Administration is the essential prerequisite for the proper functioning of any administrative justice system.

Montreal, July 5, 2010   Nour E. Benakezouh, MBA

For reasons unknown to me to this day, Dr Margaret Chan, former Director-General of WHO, felt the need to propose to me in her correspondence of 28 July 2011 to negotiate to resolve some of my complaints, which she had unilaterally selected.

I did not hesitate for a second to accept her proposal despite the traumatic experience I had with the organization during the previous three years.

I accepted Dr. Chan's offer of negotiation because negotiating comes naturally to me. I have always believed, and continue to believe to this day, that "A bad settlement is better than a good trial".

Naively, I believed that Dr. Chan had the same philosophy and that is why she had proposed to me to negotiate. The rest of the story proved, quite the opposite. I learned to my cost that the WHO did not have the same definition of the term "negotiation" as I did.

The WHO had no intention of reaching an agreement on the issues I had raised. It wanted to push through its decisions through someone it had called a negotiator without giving him any authority.

The "negotiator" found himself in an intermediary situation: I repeated my grievances to him, which I had not stopped repeating for 3 years, and he wrote them down to present them to the human resources director and hope to have answers to present them to me in turn.

I leave it to you to appreciate the "negotiation" sessions that I had the pleasure of having with Mr. Arun Seetulsingh by making available to you the email exchanges that I had with him.

From: *"Seetulsingh, Arun" <seetulsingha@who.int>*
To: *yassirem@yahoo.com*
Sent: *Thursday, September 15, 2011, 8h43*

> ***Object:*** *RE: Our discussion - Decision of the WHO Director-General-Appeal No.755 before the Headquarters Board of Appeal*

Sir,

Thank you. I have not heard from you. I hope you were able to have a moment to get back to resolving our issues.

Regarding your comments on the draft attestation, I suggest you insert your discussed changes in track changes mode to the attached document (identical to the one I sent you three weeks ago – with apologies for having previously mis transcribed your name in paragraph 3).

Upon receipt of the document with your suggestions, I will submit them to the Director of Human Resources.

Would you be available tomorrow, Friday, September 16th, at 9 am (Montreal) or Monday, September 19th, at the same time to continue our discussion on the phone?

Please accept, Sir, the assurance of my distinguished greetings.

Arun Seetulsingh | HR Specialist (Legal) | Human Resources Management, Policy and Administration of Justice.

Nour E. Benakezouh

From: *N B [mailto:yassirem@yahoo.com]*
Sent: *September 19, 2011, 13:07*
To: *Seetulsingh, Arun*

> ***Subject:*** *Re: Our discussion - Decision of the WHO Director-General - Appeal No. 755 before the Headquarters Board of Appeal*

Mr. Seetulsingh,

I am hereby sending you, by means of this email, my comments on the draft certificate that I promised you during our last telephone conversation, following your request to record in writing the clarifications that I had made orally.

I do not fully agree with your suggestion to insert my changes discussed in follow-up mode because I do not believe that it is up to me to decide on the wording of the attestation.

What I can do, however, is to mention the elements that I would like to see in this attestation so that it complies with the provisions of Article 1095 of the WHO Staff Rules and Regulations.

During our telephone conversation, I took care to ask you to use a tense other than the imperfect to talk about my responsibilities when you wrote, "Mr. Benakezouh was generally responsible for handling management issues and providing administrative support to the WHO Office in Mali."

What was missing from your draft attestation, and which is the most important element of my request concerning this section, is the quality of my work and my conduct in the exercise of my official functions.

Modern Day Slavery

As I mentioned to you during our telephone conversation, this certificate will be given to the United Nations agencies that requested it for the evaluation of my application and to other employers in order to answer their recurring questions regarding the reasons for the non-renewal of my contract.

During my stay in Bamako, I actively participated in various activities, ranging from vaccination campaigns that led to the eradication of polio in Mali to the preparation of the Global Ministerial Forum on Research for Health. I could give you an exhaustive list of these activities and the names of people who can testify to the quality of my participation.

As for my conduct in the exercise of my official functions, I could also provide you with the list of people (the Minister of Health of Mali, the former Regional Director of the WHO African Region, the Director of the United Nations Foundation, etc.) who can speak to you about my conduct.

Please accept, Mr. Seetulsingh, the expression of my distinguished greetings.

Nour E. Benakezouh, MBA, LIFA.
yassirem@yahoo.com

From: "Seetulsingh, Arun" <seetulsingha@who.int>
To: yassirem@yahoo.com
Sent: Monday, October 10, 2011, 6h00

> *Object:* Re: Our discussion - Decision of the WHO Director-General - Appeal No. 755 before the Headquarters Board of Appeal

Sir,

Following our last discussion on September 27th, I have had consultations with the Director of Human Resources. Due to a heavy workload in our department at the moment, I apologize for the time taken for these consultations. I will contact you again in the coming days to continue our discussions.

Please accept, Sir, the assurance of my distinguished greetings.

Arun Seetulsingh | HR Specialist (Legal) | Human Resources Management, Policy and Administration of Justice

From: N B [mailto:yassirem@yahoo.com]
Sent: October 12 2011 19:36
To: Seetulsingh, Arun

> *Subject:* Re: Our discussion - Decision of the WHO Director-General - Appeal No. 755 before the Headquarters Board of Appeal

Mr. Seetulsingh,

I have read the contents of your October 10th email in which you apologize for the time you took for consultations with the Director of Human Resources. Delay that you attribute to the heavy workload in your department.

Modern Day Slavery

Far from doubting for a second that your department is busy doing important things, I want to inform you that I very much doubt that the workload is the reason why our negotiations are stalling.

The fundamental premise for the success of any negotiation lies in the good faith of the parties involved. I must regretfully inform you that the World Health Organization has not, at any time during the last three years, demonstrated an ounce of good faith toward me.

When the Director-General proposed to me in her July 28th, 2011 correspondence to negotiate to resolve some of my complaints, which she had unilaterally selected, I did not hesitate one second to accept her proposal despite the traumatic experience I had with the Organization during the previous three years.

I accepted her offer of talks because, by nature, I am for negotiation. I then put the past aside and decided to respond present to the call of reason.

Two months later I realize that good faith was unfortunately, missing, once again, at the negotiation table. My minimalist request of a certificate in accordance with the provisions of Article 1095 of the Staff Regulations and Regulations in order to be able to take care of my family has not been able to find an echo in your department. My hope of being able to activate my job search during this back-to-school period has, as a result, been dashed.

The Organization is much more concerned with protecting my superior (embezzlement, lies, forgery, and use of forgery, etc.) than with repairing an injustice that has lasted too long and which risks causing serious harm to my family.

The discussions we had have, at least, one merit: That of not allowing the WHO to argue ignorance once the real reasons for the *non-renewal of my contract have been exposed one day. Divine justice has always done its work.*

Until then, I think we should reserve our efforts for the Administrative Tribunal because my convictions that anything can come out of our discussion have diminished considerably, not to say vanished.

Please accept, Mr. Seetulsingh, the expression of my distinguished greetings.

Nour E. Benakezouh, MBA, LIFA.
yassirem@yahoo.com

Modern Day Slavery

World Health Organization
20, AVENUE APPIA-CH-1211GENEVE27 -SUISSE-
www.who.int

M. Nour-Eddine Benakezouh
Montréal QC H1R 2P6
Canada

Geneva, November 7th, 2011

Sir,

In your letter dated August 8th, 2011, in response to the final decision of the WHO Director-General dated July 29th, 2011, on your appeal to the Headquarters Board of Appeal, you noted his wish for a comprehensive settlement of your dispute and indicated your support for the proposed approach, namely to examine three specific issues as a priority as detailed below.

To this end, a representative of the Human Resources Management Department had various email exchanges and telephone conversations with you. This representative reported to me, in particular, the content of the four conversations you had on the telephone with him on 17, 19, 26 August, and September 27, 2011.

I take note of your wish expressed in your email of October 17th, 2011, despite the efforts of WHO made in the context of these discussions, namely your statement that "we should reserve our efforts for (the) Administrative Tribunal" and give your preference for a judicial resolution of the dispute.

The purpose of this communication is to conclude the review of your grievances. The Director-General had asked us on July 29th, 2011, to discuss and consider the following three questions:

1. **Conditions for the evaluation of your professional services during the duration of your contract**

    The report of your supervisor concerning the performance of your duties, dated October 14th, 2008, not having been prepared in accordance with the forms applicable to performance evaluation, has been removed from your file kept by the Organization. I therefore confirm the absence of any report on the evaluation of your services during your period of assignment to the WHO Country Office in Mali.

2. **End of your temporary engagement**

    As reported to the Headquarters Board of Appeal, your temporary appointment was not extended because the position you held in the WHO Country Office in Mali was the subject of a decision to reassign a staff member on an indefinite term.

    I regret that this reason was only clearly communicated to you during the exchange of submissions before the Headquarters Board of Appeal. However, I remind you that you were aware when you accepted a temporary appointment that it did not entitle you to a new appointment with the WHO and that its duration would be limited to two years at the most.

3. **Attestation**

    I am attaching to this letter the certificate of service, the content of which you discussed on August 26 and September 27, 2011, with the representative of the Human Resources Management Department. With regard to your request that the certificate mention the quality of your work and your conduct in the exercise of your official functions, the Organization cannot grant it for the reasons that were detailed to you during the above-mentioned discussions.

Without holding you responsible for this situation, we therefore conclude that the evaluation of your performance could not be completed by your direct supervisor in accordance with the procedure in force. Please also note that persons outside the Organization cannot validly carry out such an evaluation, nor can officials who have now left their functions at the Regional Office or officials who were not your direct supervisors.

For your convenience, I recommend that you provide the contact details of the Regional Human Resources Officer, Regional Office for Africa, Mr. Makhtar Ndiaye (email: ndiayem@afro.who.int; telephone: +4724139201) if potential employers seek to interview your supervisors at WHO. If necessary, he will be able to officially confirm the content of the attached attestation to them.

As you know, you are no longer a staff member. Consequently, and in accordance with Article 1240 of the Staff Rules, as well as the case law of the ILO Administrative Tribunal, you no longer have access to the procedures for intimate appeal before the Regional Board of Appeal or the Headquarters Board of Appeal, in the event of disagreement with the content of this letter. However, you have the possibility of raising this issue before the ILO Administrative Tribunal, in accordance with its Statutes and Rules, as part of the ongoing proceedings concerning you under reference AT 5-3101.

Please accept, Sir, the assurance of my highest consideration.

Monika Altmaler

Nour E. Benakezouh
Director of Human Resources Management

Cc: Director General

RPO, AFRO

World Health Organization
20, AVENUE APPIA-CH-1211GENEVE27 -SUISSE-
www.who.int

M. Nour-Eddine Benakezouh
Montréal QC H1R 2P6
Canada

Geneva, November 7th, 2011

By this attestation, the World Health Organization (WHO) certifies that Mr. Nour-Eddine Benakezouh held the position of Administrator at the WHO Representative Office in Mali from November 10th, 2007, to December 6th, 2008.

In his capacity as Administrator, Mr. Benakezouh generally dealt with management issues and provided administrative support to the WHO Office in Mali, as well as advising WHO staff on financial, personnel, immigration and protocol matters. In particular, he was responsible:

- To assess the alignment of resources with the objectives of the WHO country program in Mali;

- To ensure contact with the national authorities of Mali and institutional counterparts on operational issues aimed at establishing relationships of trust and effective coordination and collaboration;

- To contribute to the smooth execution of the program by providing timely administrative support and advice on rules and procedures relating to financial, human resources, and infrastructure matters;

- To ensure a reliable and efficient administrative service.

Nour E. Benakezouh

During his assignment in Mali, Mr. Benakezouh activities included providing support for the monitoring and evaluation of the program; preparing draft documents and an estimate of the biennial budget; carrying out administrative tasks, particularly on financial, logistical and human resources issues, including the recruitment of temporary and support staff; coordinating, in conjunction with national authorities, administrative matters concerning staff members.

Mr. Benakezouh was actively involved in the activities of the Country Office, including vaccination campaigns aimed at eradicating polio in Mali and in the preparation of a Global Ministerial Forum on Research for Health.

Monika Altmaler

Director of Human Resources Management

Modern Day Slavery

M. Nour-Eddine Benakezouh, MBA
Montréal, QC H1R 2P6
yassirem@yahoo.com

November 29th, 2011

Mrs. Monika Altmaler
Director Human Resources Management
World Health Organization
20, Avenue Apia 1211
Genève, 27, Suisse

Dear Mrs. Altmaler,

I acknowledge receipt of your letter dated November 8th, 2011, in which you define the object in paragraph 4: **"to conclude the examination of your grievances."**

Concluding a negotiation process presumes that there have been negotiations, which is far from being the case with the exercise I had to do with the person you designated to communicate, rather than negotiate, with me since your representative, although very pleasant and professional, was content to be a sounding board, in accordance with the mandate you assigned him.

In fact, no decision-making power had been given to him in the context of this exercise. I found myself, therefore, repeating my grievances to him and him writing them down to present them to you and hoping to have answers from you so that he could present them to me.

You took care to note, in your correspondence, my desire to reserve our efforts for the Administrative Tribunal without taking the trouble to mention the reasons which led me to do so. I will take this opportunity to explain them to you, in case you don't know them which I seriously doubt.

As I mentioned in my October 17*th*, 2011 email, to which you refer in your correspondence, the fundamental premise for the success of any negotiation is the good faith of the parties concerned. The World Health Organization, contrary to what you claim in your letter, has not, at any time during the last three years, including the period of the "negotiations," demonstrated an ounce of good faith towards me.

When the Director-General proposed to me in her correspondence of July 28*th*, 2011, to negotiate to resolve some of my complaints, which she had unilaterally selected, I did not hesitate for a minute to accept her proposal despite the traumatic experience I had with the Organization during the previous three years.

I accepted her offer of talks because I am, by nature, for negotiation. I then ignored the past and decided to answer the call of reason now.

Two months later, I realize that good faith has unfortunately not been, once again, absent from the negotiation table. My minimalist request to be issued with a certificate in accordance with the provisions of Article 1095 of the Staff Regulations and Regulations in order to be able to take care of my family could not find an echo in your department. My hope of being able to activate my job search during this back-to-school period has, as a result, been dashed.

The Organization is much more concerned with protecting my superior (embezzlement, lies, forgery, and use of forgery, etc.) than with repairing an injustice that has lasted too long and which risks causing serious harm to my family.

Modern Day Slavery

I would also like to remind you that as of October 17th, 2011, the date of writing my email, to which you refer in your letter, the sixty-day deadline, set unilaterally by the Director-General, had already passed. Having gone almost 30 days (September 27th to October 17th, 2011) without responding to the questions that I had raised with your representative, while the deadline given to us was 60 days, does not allow you to state "despite the efforts made by WHO in the context of these discussions."

WHO made no effort other than to protect my superiors (embezzlement, lies, falsification of documents, forgery and use of forgery, etc.).

The organization, by acting in this way, supports actions and behaviors that go against the fundamental principles of the United Nations, of which it is a specialized agency.

The discussions I had with your representative have merit, however. That of not allowing the WHO to argue ignorance of the facts, once the reasons for the maintenance of my hierarchical superior as WHO Representative in Bamako, despite all her actions and behaviors. Officials of the WHO Representation in Mali will soon retire and will no longer be afraid to speak, which tends to loosen tongues.

The WHO will have to face a media frenzy that will be no less than that suffered by the International Monetary Fund (IMF) in the case of Mr. Dominique Strauss-Kahn (DSK).

A simple reading of your conclusions is enough to convince the common man of my assertion of lack of good faith on the part of the WHO:

1. Evaluation of my professional services

You simply say that my superior's report was not prepared in accordance with the applicable standards for performance evaluation while ignoring her defamation, her lies, and her falsification of documents. What do you do with the Organization's duty to defend the reputation of its employees? What do you do with the Organization's duty of care towards me and its duty of good management?

2. **End of my temporary engagement**

You know very well that the non-renewal of my contract has nothing to do with the reassignment of a staff member hired for an indefinite period. Your argument does not hold water, and you know it very well. It raises more questions than it tries to resolve.

One of these questions is contained in the same sentence which says one thing and its opposite: reassignment of a staff member hired for an **indefinite period to a temporary position***.*

In addition, the WHO African Region advertised 11 vacancies for administrative positions during this period, the vast majority of which were for a fixed term, not temporary. WHO could have assigned this staff member to one of these positions. This is not to mention the other contradictions that destroy the reason you gave for not renewing my contract.

3. **Attestation**

The reasons you gave for not issuing a certificate are disconcerting.

You ask me to "note furthermore that persons outside the Organization cannot validly carry out such an evaluation, nor can officials who have now left their functions at the

Regional Office OR officials who were not your direct supervisors."

I never asked you or your emissary for such a thing. I did, however, recommend Dr. Lamine Cisse Saar, who meets all the conditions to evaluate my work. He was my direct supervisor, and he did not leave his duties at the regional office.

You are asking me to pay too high a price for myself and my family because my two superiors did not do their job, lied, and falsified documents. Instead of paying the price, they are kept in their positions, even promoted to higher positions.

I must confess that I spent more than a week trying, without success, to understand the logic of this reasoning.

Please accept, Mrs. Altmaier, the expression of my distinguished greetings.

Nour E. Benakezouh

Cc: General Director WHO

> *It is not the silence of a few that scares me,*
> *It is the silence of the many*
>
> - **Martin Luther King**

I am not the only one who suffers harm when the administration does not follow its own rules as it should. The entire administrative process is, in fact, undermined when my rights to due process are seriously affected.

A scrupulous and impeccable compliance with the procedure established by the administration is the essential prerequisite for the proper functioning of any administrative justice system.

I am the first to admit that Mrs. Monika Altmaler, Director of Human Resources at the WHO Directorate-General, was in a difficult position when she had to respond to my August 8th, 2011 to the WHO Director-General. She found herself in a situation that I would not wish on my worst enemy.

The WHO management had chosen not to address the issue of Modern-Day Slavery, of lying, of falsification of documents, and of misappropriation of funds of the WHO representation in Bamako by Dr. Fatoumata Binta Diallo. This choice was dictated by the fact that the WHO Regional Director for Africa, Dr. Luis Gomes Sambo, was part of the plot. WHO became, by transitiveness, part of the same plot.

Once the decision to turn its back on humanism and justice was taken by the general management of the WHO, a specialized agency of the United Nations, initiator and adopter of the Universal Declaration of Human Rights, Mrs. Altmaler had the mission to do everything to avoid talking about this collusion. She found herself, because of that, dancing around the bush, talking about everything and nothing in her November 7th, 2011 letter.

To reach her destination, Mrs. Altmaler was forced to take several paths: the path of lies, the path of misinterpreting the articles of the regulations, and the path of not citing the judgment numbers to which she cheerfully alluded in her correspondence.

In addressing the issue of the submission of an evaluation full of lies and false documents by my superior, Mrs. Altmaler merely states, *"The report of your superior concerning the exercise of your functions, dated October 14th, 2008, not having been established in accordance with the forms applicable to performance evaluation, was removed from your file kept by the Organization. I therefore confirm the absence of any report on the evaluation of your services during your period of assignment to the WHO Country Office in Mali."*

One must admit that this is a revolutionary way of solving problems: **Dr. Diallo resorts to lies, defamation, and falsification of documents, and it is Mr. Benakezouh who pays the price for all this**. The WHO should patent this way of doing things.

For reasons that are too obvious, Mrs. Altmaler never really asked herself the questions about why this happened and what the consequences were for my superior because the answer to these kinds of questions would lead directly to talking about the Modern-Day Slavery of the little Angolan girl. And since talking about the Modern-Day Slavery of the little Angolan girl is not and should never be on the agenda, Mrs. Altmaler had no choice but to make a fool of herself.

As for the non-renewal of my contract, Mrs. Altmaler regrets that the reason was not clearly communicated to me until the exchange of submissions before the Appeals Committee of the Headquarters.

Mrs. Altmaler forgot to say that the reason for the non-renewal of my contract was the best kept secret of the WHO for three years and two days, from November 5th, 2008, to November 7th, 2011, despite my 33 correspondences in which I wanted to know this reason. The World Health Organization finally decided to give birth to the so-called reason for the non-renewal of my contract after 36 months and 2 days of pregnancy.

Even when she was forced to give the reason for the non-renewal of my contract, Mrs. Altmaler was unable, to tell the truth because, once again, telling the truth would force her to answer the awkward questions: the question of the little Angolan girl and that of Modern-Day Slavery within the WHO.

Mrs. Altmaler, with no shame, states in her letter, *"Your temporary appointment was not extended because the position you occupied at the WHO Country Office in Mali was the subject of a decision to reassign a staff member hired for an indefinite period."*

Reading her response, one cannot help but ask the following question: **What is a staff member hired for an indefinite period doing in a temporary position**? It is practically impossible to answer this question when we know that the WHO African Region advertised 11 vacancies for professional positions during this period, the vast majority of which were for a fixed term, therefore not temporary. WHO could have assigned this staff member to one of these positions.

Once launched into the lie, nothing and no one could stop Mrs. Altmaler, who took the care to ask me, "Please note also that people outside the organization cannot validly carry out such an evaluation, nor can officials who have now left their functions at the Regional Office OR officials who were not YOUR direct supervisors."

This passage was certainly not addressed to me since I never suggested to her to call on people outside the Organization to do my evaluation. I never asked Mrs. Altmaler or her emissary for such a thing. I did, however, recommend Dr. Lamine Cisse Saar to her. Dr. Saar meets all the conditions to evaluate my work. He was my direct supervisor, and he did not leave his functions at the regional office.

The Director of Human Resources Management of WHO had asked me to pay a price that was too high for me and my family because my two superiors did not do their job, lied, and falsified documents. Instead of them to pay the price; they are kept in their positions or even promoted to higher positions.

All the sacrifices that had been asked of me by the general management had only one objective: To cover up the Modern-Day Slavery of the little Angolan girl in order to save the WHO regional director for Africa.

The WHO's behavior, in this case, is inspired by the American film by Steven Spielberg, "**Saving Private Ryan.**" Ryan is Dr Gomez L. Sambo, Regional Director of WHO for Africa.

A man does what he must in spite of personal consequences, obstacles, dangers, and pressures; and that is the basis of all human morality

- John F. Kennedy

I often ask myself the question of whether I would have done the same thing if I was given the chance to deal with the situation once again. My answer to myself has always been: "Without the slightest hesitation," because I cannot close my eyes when I go to bed if I agree to close those same eyes to Modern-Day Slavery and the rape of minors.

Does this mean that I don't regret some of the things I did? Not at all; I have a lot of regrets but no remorse. I have no remorse because everything I did, I did it consciously, in good faith, and with the information and knowledge of the moment.

As for regrets, I especially regret having made my two children, Tarik & Assirem, pay the price for my convictions. They had done nothing to deserve this. I take this opportunity to apologize to them once again and to tell them that their father could not live a life as an accomplice to slavery, whatever form it took.

I regret not having freed the little Angolan girl who found herself a modern-day slave because her father believed at one point that he had made the best decision by letting her go to Bamako with Dr Diallo. He dreamed of a better future for his daughter by acting in that way. He probably never believed that his daughter would not attend school.

I also regret the fact that this experience has made me lose faith in the United Nations and its agencies. Never, ever, would I have believed that such a story could take place in the 21st century within a specialized agency of the United Nations whose main objective is to build a better future for the people of the world.

My thoughts go to the little Angolan girl who was the victim of Dr. Diallo's behavior and especially of the complicit silence of all the WHO leaders who had chosen to turn a blind eye for one reason or another and when they were informed of the situation, they chose to dance around the bush.

I always wondered if they could close their eyes at night as they did in broad daylight. I also wondered if their conscience demands accountability or if they murdered it. For my part, I have always been inspired by Victor Hugo, in this chapter, when he says: **"Better a clear conscience than a prosperous destiny. I prefer a good sleep to a good bed."**

To maintain their privileges, these leaders made sacrifices, and the most important thing they sacrificed was their thirst for human dignity. By sacrificing the latter, these leaders made an organization, that needed it so badly to achieve its main objective, lose all trustworthiness.

This lack of standing was felt strongly during the COVID-19 vaccination campaign. I had to talk to people from various backgrounds, nationalities, and religions about why they did not want to get vaccinated. The number one reason for this refusal was the lack of credibility in the WHO leadership. The vast majority of people I had discussed the vaccine with had no quarrel with science.

For the sake of humanity, I hope that future generations of WHO leaders will no longer tolerate modern-day slavery within their institution.

I cannot ignore the silence of Canada's political leaders from all parties in the face of this case of Modern-Day Slavery.

Two days after my return to Canada, on Wednesday, December November 17th, 2008, I sent a letter to the Honorable Leona Aglukkaq, Minister of Health, with a copy to the Honorable Steven Harper, Prime Minister of Canada, and the Honorable Michaëlle Jean, Governor General of Canada.

In the letter, I had detailed the modern-day slavery that was taking place in the open in an organization where:

1. Canada is a member of the Executive Council;
2. Canada has been a strong supporter of the WHO since its creation in 1948;
3. Minister of Health leads the Canadian delegation to the annual World Health Assembly, WHO's top decision-making body.

I didn't even get an acknowledgment letter from any of the leaders I listed above.

Not having learned my lesson or, rather, not wanting to learn my lesson, I did the same exercise again in 2023. In addition to the Minister of Health, the Prime Minister, and the Governor General, this time I added Mr. Nicolas Palanque, Executive Director of the Public Health Agency of Canada, and a a member of the WHO Executive Board.

I received:

- An acknowledgment of receipt from the Minister of Health;
- A correspondence from the Prime Minister's office;
- A total contempt on the part of the Governor General of Canada;
- A total contempt on the part of Mr. Nicolas Palanque, Executive Director of the Public Health Agency of Canada, in his capacity as a member of the WHO Executive Board.

The response from the office of the Honorable Prime Minister of Canada is so unique that I have no other choice than to share it.

On February 11, 2023, I sent the following email to the Office of the Honorable Justin Trudeau, Prime Minister of Canada.

From: nour.benakezouh@outlook.com
Received: 11 February, 2023 09:57:19 AM
Subject: Health

Date: 2023/02/11 2:56:48 PM
Comments: Honorable Justin Trudeau,

My name is Nour-Eddine Benakezouh and I am Canadian. I worked as an administrator in the WHO representation in Bamako (Mali).

On October 1st, 2021, following the indictment of WHO by an independent commission of inquiry into sexual violence committed by some of its employees against dozens of people in the democratic Republic of Congo, I wrote a letter to the Director-General of WHO to bring to his attention a case of sexual exploitation and abuse within the WHO representation in Bamako that I had the misfortune to experience as a witness and which was the cause of my loss of job because I naively brought to the attention of the Director of Administration and Finance (DAF) of the WHO Africa directorate, the actions of the WHO representative in Bamako: Dr. Fatoumata Binta T. Diallo.

On October 6th, 2021, I received a letter from Ms. Cristiana Fascetto, Investigator, Office of Internal Oversight Services (IOS), informing me: "Your letter of October 1 to the Director-General has been forwarded to our office. As the allegations you reported are very serious, we have proceeded to immediately open an investigation."

Seeing nothing happen, I sent a second letter to the WHO Director-General on December 18th, 2022, to inform him of the progress of the investigation opened by WHO on October 6th, 2021.

Having received no news to date, not even an acknowledgment of receipt, from the Director-General of the WHO, I have decided to contact you in the hope of putting an end to a situation that has lasted far too long.

My sincere greetings

The response from the Office of the Honorable Prime Minister of Canada was not long in coming. On February 14, I received an email from Richer, who did not consider it necessary to include his first name, which said the following:

De: *Prime Minister <PM@pm.gc.ca>*
Sent: *14 February 2023 15:03*
To: *nour.benakezouh@outlook.com*

Object: *Office of the Prime Minister*

Mister,

On behalf of Prime Minister Justin Trudeau, I acknowledge receipt of your correspondence regarding your former employment with the WHO.

Thank you for taking the time to write. While we can assure you that we have noted your comments, we are unfortunately unable to assist you in as this matter doesn't fall under federal jurisdiction.

Regret that my response cannot be favorable.

Thank you again for writing to the Prime Minister.

Mr. Richer
Correspondence Officer
for Senior Management

Surprised by the content and style of the response from the Prime Minister's office, I responded to this email the next day. I sent him the letter below:

M. Nour-Eddine Benakezouh, MBA, LIFA
Montreal, Quebec, Canada
nour.benakezouh@outlook.com

February 15th, 2023

M. Richer
Senior Management Correspondence Officer
80, rue Wellington
Ottawa, ON K1A 0A2
M. Richer,

I acknowledge receipt of your February 14th, 2023 email in response to my correspondence to the Prime Minister of Canada.

I would like to thank you for your prompt response, even though it was not appropriate.

Indeed, contrary to what you state in the first sentence of your email, the subject of my correspondence is not my former job but rather sexual exploitation and abuse within the WHO.

I must respectfully admit that I am astounded to read you state that you cannot assist me in this matter because it does not fall under federal jurisdiction.

If the issue of sexual exploitation and abuse within WHO is not under federal jurisdiction, what is Mr. Nicolas Palanque, Executive Director of the Public Health Agency of Canada, doing within the WHO Executive Board, which is tasked with advising the World Health Assembly of Member States - the Organization's decision-making body - and implementing its decisions?

If the issue of sexual exploitation and abuse within the WHO is not a federal matter, how do you explain the fact that Canada is one of the 57 countries on whose behalf British Ambassador Simon Manley issued a statement expressing "deep concern" about these accusations of sexual exploitation and abuse within the WHO?

The 57 countries, including Canada, called for a victim- and survivor-centered approach. "Complaints must be addressed promptly, and perpetrators held accountable, and we strongly support efforts to strengthen the WHO's investigative capacity."

As a victim of sexual exploitation and abuse within the WHO, I had addressed my correspondence to my first ministry.

I take this opportunity to send you some of the documents proving my allegations.

My sincere greetings.

Nour E. Benakezouh, MBA, LIFA

Needless to say, I have not received any response to date to my letter. This contempt is probably the reason why citizens have lost confidence in their leaders.

In light of everything I have experienced since November 10th, 2007, I have come to the conclusion that politics and health do not mix.

Nour E. Benakezouh

Every person exists as an end in themselves, and not merely as a means to be used at someone's discretion.

- Emanuel Kant

In January 2025, I have to go, once again, to the same operating room of the same hospital to undergo another back operation in the hands of the same orthopedist, Dr Ahmed Aoude, whom I would like to thank for everything he has done for me since January 2021.

This time, I wouldn't be surprised if the little Angolan girl decided to accompany me to the operating room. I dream and I would be delighted to see her accompany me to the operating room because this time I could look her in the eye to tell her that I kept my promise.

I also wish to have my two children, Tarik and Assirem, by my side to ask them for forgiveness, once again, for what I have done to them. I hope that one day they will understand that I had no choice but to do what I did. I hope that they will never have to go through what I have gone through. They deserve better than this from life and I think that I have paid the price for the whole family.

My friends often ask me if I wasn't afraid to take on the World Health Organization. My answer has not changed one iota since April 2008, when I decided to do everything humanly possible to preserve my dignity by first refusing to be complicit in modern-day slavery and the rape of minors and then by exposing the perpetrators and those who chose to turn a blind eye.

I never thought that by doing this I was attacking the World Health Organization as an institution. I resist and will resist, until the

Modern Day Slavery

last day of my life, modern-day slavery and the sexual rape of minors.

If the WHO leadership has chosen to turn a blind eye to modern-day slavery and/or the rape of minors within its institution, I have no choice but to point the finger at the organization that shelters the modern-day slavery and the rape of minors.